William Jones

The Design of Enslaving England Discovered

Being a new corrected impression of that excellent piece intituled. A just

and modest vindication of the proceedings of the two last Parliaments of

King Charles the Second

William Jones

The Design of Enslaving England Discovered
Being a new corrected impression of that excellent piece intituled. A just and modest vindication of the proceedings of the two last Parliaments of King Charles the Second

ISBN/EAN: 9783337409456

Printed in Europe, USA, Canada, Australia, Japan

Cover: Foto ©ninafisch / pixelio.de

More available books at **www.hansebooks.com**

THE

Defign of Enflaving *ENGLAND*

DISCOVERED.

THE

Defign of Enflaving *ENGLAND*

DISCOVERED

In the Incroachments upon the Powers
and Privileges of Parliament, by K. *Charles* II.

BEING

A New corrected Impreffion of that Excellent Piece,

INTITULED,

A Juft and Modeft VINDICATION of the

PROCEEDINGS

OF THE

Two Laft Parliaments

OF

King *CHARLES* the Second.

LONDON;
Printed for Richard Baldwin near the Black Bull
in the *Old-Baily*. MDCLXXXIX.

A *Juſt and Modeſt Vindication of the Proceedings of the two laſt* Parliaments *of K.* Charles *the Second.*

THE Amazement which ſeiz'd every good Man upon the unlook'd-for Diſſolution of two Parliaments, within three Months, was not greater than at the ſight of a Declaration pretending to juſtify, and give Reaſons for ſuch extraordinary Proceedings.

It is not to be denied, but that our Kings have in a great meaſure been intruſted by the Kingdom with the appointment of the Times of Parliaments Sitting, and declaring their Diſſolutions. But left through defect of Age, Experience, or Underſtanding, they ſhould at any time forget, or miſtake our Conſtitution ; or by Paſſion, private Intereſt, or the Influence of ill Counſellors, be ſo far miſled as not to Aſſemble Parliaments when the Publick Affairs require it ; or to declare them Diſſolved, before the Ends of their Meeting were accompliſhed : The Wiſdom of our Anceſtors has provided, by divers Statutes, both for the holding Parliaments annually, and oftner if need be ; and that they ſhould not be Prorogued or Diſſolved till all the Petitions and Bills before them were anſwered and redreſſed.

4 Edw. 3
35 Ed. 3.
*See the 1
ment Roll
2 Ric. 2
num. 28
See the ſ
modo tei
Parliamei

The Conſtitution had been equally imperfect and deſtructive of it ſelf, had it been left to the Will and Choice of the Prince whether he would ever ſummon a Parliament, or put into his Power to diſmiſs them Arbitrarily at his pleaſure.

That Parliaments ſhould be called, and ſit, according to the Laws, is ſecured to us by the ſame Sacred Tie, by which the King at his Coronation obliges himſelf, to let his Judges ſit to diſtribute Juſtice every Term, and to preſerve inviolably all other Rights and Liberties of his Subjects. Therefore abruptly to Diſſolve Parliaments at ſuch a Time, when nothing but

A   the

the Legiſlative Power, and the united Wiſdom of the Kingdom could relieve us from our Juſt Fears, or ſecure us from
our certain Dangers, is very unſuitable to the great Truſt re-
poſed in the Prince, and ſeems to expreſs but little of that affection which we will always hope his Majeſty bears towards his
People and the Proteſtant Religion.

But 'tis not only of the Diſſolution it ſelf that we complain ;
the manner of doing it, is unwarranted by the Precedents of
former Times, and full of dangerous Conſequents. We are
taught by the Writ of Summons, that Parliaments are never
called without the Advice of the Council; and the Uſage of all
Ages has been never to ſend them away without the ſame Advice. To forſake this ſafe Method, is to expoſe the King perſonally to the Reflections and Cenſures of the whole Nation
for ſo ungrateful an Action.

Our Laws have taken care to make the King always dear to
his People, and to preſerve his Perſon Sacred in their Eſteem,
by wiſely preventing him from appearing as Author of any
thing which may be unacceptable to them. 'Tis therefore that
he doth not Execute any conſiderable Act of Regal Power, till it
be firſt debated and reſolved in Council, becauſe then 'tis the
Counſellors muſt anſwer for the Advice they give, and are pu-
niſhable for ſuch Orders as are Irregular and Illegal.

Nor can his Miniſters juſtify any unlawful Action under the
colour of the King's Commands, ſince all his Commands that
are contrary to Law, are void ; (which is the true Reaſon of
that well-known *Maxim*, *That the King can do no Wrong*). A
Maxim juſt in it ſelf, and alike ſafe for the Prince, and for the
Subject, there being nothing more abſurd, than that a Favourite ſhould excuſe his enormous Actings by a pretended Com-
mand, which we may reaſonably ſuppoſe he firſt procured to
be laid upon himſelf : But we know not whom to charge with
Adviſing this laſt Diſſolution : It was a Work of Darkneſs ;
and if we are not miſinform'd, the Privy Council was as much
ſurpriz'd at it as the Nation.

Nor will a future Parliament be able to charge any Body, as
the Author or Adviſer of the late printed Paper, which bears
the Title of *His Majeſty's Declaration*, though every good Subject ought to be careful how he calls it ſo. For his Majeſty
never ſpeaks to his People as a King, but either perſonally in
his

his Parliament, or at other times under his Seal, for which the Chancellor, or other Officers are refponfible, if what paffes them be not warranted by Law. Nor can the Direction of the Privy Council, enforce any thing upon the People, unlefs that Royal and Legal Stamp gives it an Authority. But this Declaration comes abroad without any fuch Sanction, and there is no other Ground to afcribe it to his Majefty, than the uncertain Credit of the Printer, whom we will eafily fufpect of an Impofture, rather than think the King would deviate from the approved courfe of his Illuftrious Anceftors, to purfue a New and Unfuccesful Method.

The firft Declaration of this fort which I ever met with, being that which was publifhed in the Year 1628 ; which was fo far from anfwering the Ends of its coming out, that it filled the whole Kingdom with Jealoufies, and was one of the firft fad Caufes of the enfuing unhappy War.

The Truth is, Declarations to juftify what Princes do, muft always be either needlefs or ineffectual. Their Actions ought to be fuch as may recommend themfelves to the World, and carry their own Evidence along with them of their ufefulnefs to the Publick ; and then no Arts to juftifiy them will be neceffary. When a Prince defcends fo low as to give his Subjects Reafons for what he has done, he not only makes them Judges whether there be any weight in thofe Reafons, but by fo unufual a fubmiffion gives caufe to fufpect, that he is confcious to himfelf that his Actions want an Apology. And if they are indeed unjuftifiable, if they are oppofite to the Inclinations, and apparently deftructive of the Intereft of his Subjects, it will be very difficult for the moft Eloquent or Infinuating Declaration, to make them in love with fuch things. And therefore they did certainly undertake no eafy Task in pretending to perfwade Men who fee themfelves expofed to the reftlefs Malice of their Enemies, who obferve the languifhing Condition of the Nation, and that nothing but a Parliament can provide Remedies for the great Evils which they Feel and Fear ; that two feveral Parliaments, upon whom they had placed all their hopes, were fo fuddenly broken, out of kindnefs to them, or with any regared to their Advantage. It was generally believed, that this Age would not have feen another Declaration, fince * *Coleman*'s was fo unluckily publifhed before its time : Not only becaufe thereby the
A 2   World

World was taught how little they ought to rely upon the fincerity of fuch kind of Writings ; but becaufe that was a Mafterpiece which could hardly be equall'd, and our prefent Minifters may well be out of Countenance, to fee their Copy fall fo very much fhort of the Original.

But fhould this Declaration be fuffered to go abroad any longer, under the Royal Name, yet it will never be thought to have proceeded from his Majefties Inclination, or his Judgment, but to be gained from him by the Artifices of the fame ill Men, who not being content to have prevailed with him to Diffolve two Parliaments, only to proteft them from publick Juftice, do now hope to excufe themfelves from being thought the Authors of that Counfel, by making him openly to avow it. But they have difcovered themfelves to the Kingdom, and have told their own Names, when they number amongft the great Crimes of the Houfe of Commons, their having *Declared divers Eminent Perfons to be Enemies to the King and Kingdom.*

'Tis our happinefs that the Cunning of thefe *Eminent Perfons* is not equal to their Malice, in that they fhould thus unwarily make themfelves known when they had fo fecretly, and with fo much Caution, given the pernicious Advice. None could be offended at the proceedings of the Parliaments, but they who were obnoxious ; none could be concerned to vindicate the Diffolution, but they who had advifed it. But they have performed this laft Undertaking after fuch a fort, that they have left themfelves not only without Juftification, but without all pretence hereafter. The People were willing to think it the Unfortunate Effect of fome fuddain and precipitate Refolution ; but fince they have now publickly affured us, that it was the Refult of Counfel and Deliberation, they cannot blame us for hoping one day to fee Juftice done upon fuch Counfellors.

But though to the Difhonour of our Country it does appear, that fome *Englifh*-men were concerned in the unhappy Advice of breaking the two laft Parliaments, and fetting up this pretended Defence of it ; yet the *Gallifcims* which are found in the Paper, fhew the Writer to have been of another Nation, or at leaft to have had his Thoughts fo much taken up for the Interefts of *France* (whilft he was labouring this way to heighten and perpetuate the Differences between the King and his People) that he could not exprefs himfelf in any other *Idiom* than theirs,

he

he would not otherwise have introduced the King, saying, That *it was a Matter extreamly sensible to Us* ; a Form of Speech peculiar to the *French*, and unknown to any other Nation. The Reader (who understands that Language) will observe so many more of this kind, as will give him just cause to doubt, whether the whole Paper was not a Translation, and whether the *English* one, or that which was published in *French*, was the Original?

Let us then no longer wonder, that the time of Dissolving our Parliaments, is known at *Paris* sooner than at *London*, since 'tis probable, the Orders now given for it, were formed there too. The Peers at *Oxford* were so totally ignorant of the Council, that they never once thought of a Dissolution till they heard it pronounced ; but the Dutchess of *Mazarine* had better Intelligence, and published the News at St. *James*'s many hours before it was done. The Declaration was not communicated to the Privy Council, till *Friday* the 8th. of *April*, when his Majesty (according to the late Method) did graciously declare to them his pleasure, to set it forth, without desiring from them any Advice in the matter ; but Monsieur *Barillon*, the *French* Ambassador, did not only read it to a Gentleman the fifth of *April*, but advised with him about it, and demanded his Opinion of it, which his Excellency will the better remember, because of the great Liberty which the Person took in ridiculing it to his Face. *Good God! to what a Condition is this Kingdom reduced, when the Ministers and Agents of the only Prince in the World, who can have Designs against, or of whom we ought to be afraid, are not only made acquainted with the most secret Passages of State, but are made our Chief Ministers too, and have the principal Conduct of our Affairs.* And let the World judg if the Commons had not reason for their Vote, when they declared those *Eminent Persons*, who manage things at this rate, *To be the Enemies to the King and Kingdom, and Promoters of the* French *Interest.*

Whosoever considers the Actions of our Great Men, will not think it strange that they should be hard put to it to find out Reasons which they might give for any of them, and they have had very ill luck whenever they went about it. That Reason which they had given for Dissolving three several Parliaments successively, is now grown ridiculous, *That the King was resolved to meet his People, and to have their Advice in frequent Parliaments.*

ments, since every Man took notice, that as soon as the Ministers began to suspect that his Majesty was inclined to hearken to, and pursue their Advice, those very Parliaments were presently Dissolved. This was all the Ground and Cause, which was thought of for breaking the last Parliament at *Westminster*, when the Proclamation of the 18*th* of *January*, 1680, was published ; but they have now considerred better, and have found out faults enough to swell into a Declaration ; and yet as much offended as they are with this Parliament, they seem more highly angry with that which followed at *Oxford*.

Nor is it at all strange that it should fall out so : For the Court never did yet Dissolve a Parliament abruptly, and in a Heat, but they found the next Parliament more averse, and to infist upon the same things with greater eagerness than the former. *English* Spirits refent no Affronts so highly as those which are done to their Representatives ; and the Court will be sure to find the Effects of that Resentment in the next Election. A Parliament does ever participate of the present Temper of the People. Never were Parliaments of more different Complexions than that of 1640, and that of 1661. Yet they both exactly answered the Humours which were predominant in the Nation, when they were respectively chosen. And therefore while the People do so universally hate and fear *France* and *Popery*, and do so well understand who they are who promote the *French* and *Popish* Interests, the Favourites do but cozen themselves to think that they will ever send up Representatives less zealous to bring them to Justice, than those against whom this Declaration is published. For surely this Declaration (what great things soever may be expected from it) will make but very few Converts, not only because it represents things as high Crimes, which the whole Kingdom has been celebrating as meritorious Actions, but because the People have been so often deceived by former Declarations, that whatsoever carries that Name, will have no Credit with them for the future. They have not yet forgotten the Declaration from *Breda*, though others forgot it so soon, and do not spare to say, that if the same Diligence, the same earnest Solicitation, had been made use of in that Affair, which have been since exercised directly contrary to the Design of it, there is no doubt but every part of it would have had the desired Success,

Succefs, and all his Majefty's Subjects would have enjoyed the Fruits of it, and have now been extolling a Prince fo careful to keep facred his Promifes to the People.

If we did take notice of the feveral Declarations, publifhed fince that which we have laft mentioned, we fhall find they figni'ic as little; and therefore we will only remember the laft, made the 20th of *April* 1679, and declared in Council and in Parliament, and after publifhed to the whole Nation : Wherein his Majefty owns that he is *fenfible of the ill pofture of his Affairs, and the great Jealoufies and Diffatisfaction of his good Subjects, whereby the Crown and Government was become too weak to preferve it felf, which proceeded from his ufe of a fingle Miniftry, and of private Advices ; and therefore profeffes his Refolution, to lay them wholly afide for the future, and to be advifed by thofe able and worthy Perfons, whom he had then chofen for his Council, in all his weighty and important Affairs.* But every Man muft acknowledg that either his Majefty has utterly forgotten this publick and folemn Promife, or elfe that nothing *weighty and important* has happen'd from that time to this very day.

As for the Declaration read in our Churches the other day, there needs no other Argument to make us doubt of the reality of the Promifes which it makes, then to confider how partially, and with how little fincerity the things which it pretends to relate, are therein reprefented. It begins with telling us in His Majefty's Name, That *it was with exceeding great Trouble that he was brought to Diffolve the two laft Parliaments, without more benefit to the People by the calling of them.* We fhould queftion his Majefty's Wifdom, did we not believe him to have underftood, that never Parliaments had greater *Opportunities* of doing good to himfelf and to his People. He could not but be fenfible of the Dangers, and of the Neceffities of his Kingdom ; and therefore could not *without exceeding great Trouble,* be prevailed upon for the fake of a few defperate Men (whom he thought himfelf concern'd to love now, only becaufe he had loved them too well, and trufted them too much before ;) not only to difappoint the Hopes and Expectations of his own People, but of almoft *Europa.* His Majefty did indeed *do his part,* fo far, in *giving Opportunities of providing for our Good,* as the calling of Parliaments does amount to, and it is to be imputed to the Minifters only,

only, *that the fuccefs* of them *did not anfwer His* and Our *Ex-pcctations.*

'Tis certain it cannot be imputed to any of the Proceedings of either of thofe Parliament; which were compofed of Men of as good Sence and Quality as any in the Nation, and pro-ceeded with as great Moderation and manag:d their Debates with as much temper as was ever known in any Parliament. If they feem'd to go too far in any thing, His Majefty's Speeches or Declarations had mifled them, by fome of which they had been invited to enter into every one of thofe Debates, to which fo much Exception has been fince taken.

Speech 21.
Octob. 1680.

Did he not frequently recommend the *Profecution of the Plot* to them, *with a ftrict and impartial Inquiry?* Did he not tell them, *That he neither thought himfeif nor them fafe, till that mat-ter was gone through with?*

Speech 30.
Apr. 1679.

Did he not in his Speech of the 30th of *April* 1679, affure them, that it was *his conftant Care to fecure our Religion for the future in all Events, and that in all things which cencern'd the publick Security, he would not follow their Zeal but lead it?* Has he not often wifh'd, *that he might be able to exercife a Power of Difpenfation in reference to thofe Proteftants, who through Tendernefs of mifguided Confcience did not conform to the Ceremonies, Difci-pline and Government of the Church?* And promifed that he would *make it his fpecial Care to incline the Wifdom of the Parlia-ment to concur with him, in making an Act to that purpofe?*

Speech 26.
Dec. 1662.

And left the Malice of ill Men might object, that thefe Graci-ous Inclinations of his continued no longer, than while there was a poffibility of giving the Papifts equal benefit of a Tolera-tion; Has not his Majefty, fince the Difcovery of the Plot, fince there was no hopes of getting fo much as a Convenience for them, in his Speech of the 6th of *March* 1679, expreft *his Zeal* not only *for the Proteftant Religion in general, but for an Union amongft all forts of Proteftants?* And did he not com-mand my Lord Chancellor at the fame time to tell them, *that it was neceffary to diftinguifh between Popifh and other Recufants, between them that would deftroy the whole Flock, and them that on-ly wander from it?*

Speech 6.
March 1679.

Thefe things confidered, we fhould not think the Parliament went too far, but rather that they did not follow his Majefty's Zeal with an equal pace. The Truth is, if we obferve the dai-ly

ly provocations of the Popish Faction, whose Rage and Info-
lence were only increased by the Discovery of the Plot; so
that they seemed to defy Parliaments, as well as Inferior Courts
of Justice, under the Protection of the Duke, (their publickly
avowed Head); who still carried on their Designs by new and
more detestable Methods than ever, and were continually busy,
by Perjuries and Subornations, to charge the best and most con-
siderable Protestants in the Kingdom with Treasons, as black as
those of which themselves were guilty. If we observe what
vile Arts were used to hinder the further Discovery, what Liberty was given to reproach the Discoverers, what Means used
to destroy or to corrupt them; how the very Criminals were
encouraged and allowed to be good Witnesses against their Ac-
cusers: We should easily excuse any *English* Parliament thus
beset, if they had been carried to some little Excesses. But yet
all this could not provoke them to do any thing not justifiable
by the Laws of Parliament, or unbecoming the Wisdom and
Gravity of an *English* Senate.

But we are told, That his Majesty *Opened the last Parliament,
which was held at* Westminster, *with as Gracious Expressions of
His Readiness to satisfy the Desires of his Subjects, and to secure
hem against all their just Fears, as the Weighty Consideration,
ither of preserving the Established Religion and Property of his
subjects at Home, or of supporting his Neighbours and Allies A-
road, could fill his Heart with.* We must own that his Ma-
esty has Opened all his Parliaments at *Westminster,* with very
racious Expressions: Nor have wanted that Evidence of His
eadiness to satisfy the Desires of his Subjects; but that sort of
Evidence will soon lose its Force, if it be never followed by
Actions correspondent, by which only the World can judg of
the sincerity of Expressions or Intentions. And therefore the
Favourites did little consult his Majesty's Honour, when they
bring him in solemnly declaring to his Subjects, *That his Intentions were as far as would have consisted with the very Being of
the Government, to have complied with any thing that could have been
proposed to him to accomplish those Ends;* when they are not able
to produce an Instance wherein they suffered him to comply in
any one Thing. Whatsoever the House of Commons Ad-
dress'd for, was certainly denied, though it was only for that
Reason; and there was no surer way of Intituling ones self to

B the

the Favour of the Court, than to receive a Censure from the Representative Body of the People.

Let it for the present be admitted, that some of the things desired by that Parliament were exorbitant, and (because we will put the Objection as strong as is possible) inconsistent with the very being of the Government; yet at least, some of their Petitions were more reasonable. The Government might have subsisted, tho the Gentlemen, put out of the Commission of the Peace, for their zealous acting against the Papists, had been restor'd ; nor would a final Dissolution of all things have ensued, tho Sir *George Jefferies* had been removed out of publick Office, or my Lord *Hallifax* himself from his Majesty's Presence and Councils. Had the Statute of the 35 *Eliz.* (which had justly slept for Eighty Years, and of late, unseasonably revived) been repealed, surely the Government might still have been safe. And tho the Fanaticks perhaps had not deserved so well as that in favour to them, his Majesty should have passed that Bill; yet since the Repeal might hereafter be of so great use to those of the Church of *England*, in case of a Popish Successor, (which Blessing his Majesty seems resolved to bequeath to his People); one would have thought he might have complied with the Parliament in that Proposal. At least, we should have had less reason to complain of the Refusal, if the King would have been but graciously pleased to have done it in the ordinary way.

But the Ministers thought they had not sufficiently triumphed over the Parliament, by getting the Bill rejected, unless it were done in such a manner as that the President might be more pernicious to Posterity, by introducing a new *Negative* in the making of Laws, than the losing of any Bill, how useful soever, could be to the present Age. This we may affirm, that if the Success of this Parliament did not answer Expectation, whoever was guilty of it, the House of Commons did not fail of *doing their Part*. Never did Men husband their time to more Advantage. They opened the Eyes of the Nation; They shewed them their Danger, with a Freedom becoming Englishmen. They asserted the Peoples Right of Petitioning : They proceeded vigorously against the Conspirators Discovered, and heartily endeavoured to take away the very Root of the Conspiracy : They had before them as many great and useful Bills as had been seen in any Parliament, and it is not to be laid at

their

their doors that they proved Abortive. This Age will never fail to give them their grateful Acknowledgments, and Posterity will remember that House of Commons with Honour.-

We come now to the particular enumeration of those gracious Things which were said to the Parliament at *Westminster*. His Majesty ask'd of them *the supporting the Alliances he had made for the Preservation of the general Peace in Christendom.* 'Tis to be wish'd his Majesty had added to this gracious Asking of Mony, a gracious Communication of those Alliances, and that such blind Obedience had not been exacted from them, as to contribute to the Support of they knew not what themselves ; nor before they had considered whether those Alliances which were made, were truly design'd for that End which was pretended, or any way likely to prove effectual to it. Since no Precedent can be shewn, that ever a Parliament (not even the late Long Parliament, though filled with *Danby's* Pensioners) did give Mony for maintaining any Leagues, till they were first made acquainted with the particulars of them.

But besides this, the Parliament had reason to consider well of the general Peace it self, and the Influence it might have, and had upon our Affairs, before they came to any Resolution, or so much as to a Debate about preserving it ; since so wise a Minister as my Lord *Chancellor* had so lately told us, *That it was fitter for Meditation than Discourse.* -- He informed us in the same Speech, That the Peace then was but the Effect of Despair in the Confederates; and we have since learn'd by whose means they were reduced to that Despair ; and what Price was demanded of the *French* King for so great a Service. And we cannot but be sadly sensible how by this Peace, that Monarch has not only quite Dissolv'd the Confederacy form'd against him, enlarged his Dominions, gain'd time to refresh his Souldiers harrassed with long Service, settled and composed his Subjects at home, increased his Fleet, and replenished his Exchequer for new and greater Designs ; but his Pensioners at our Court have grown insolent upon it, and presuming that now he may be at leisure to assist them in ruining *England*, and the Protestant Religion together, have shaken off all dread of Parliaments, and have prevail'd with his Majesty to use them with as little respect, and to disperse them with as great Contempt, as if they had been a Conventicle, and not the great Representative of the Nation, whose Power and

Lord Chancellor's Speech, 2 *May,* 1578.

Wisdom

Wifdom only could fave him and us, in our prefent Exigencies.

But whatever the Defign of them was, or the Effect of them
is like to be, yet Alliances have a very good found, and a Nation fo encompaffed with Enemies abroad, and Traitors and
Penfioners to thofe Enemies at home, muft needs be glad to
hear of any new Friends. But alas, if we look into the Speech
made at the Opening of that Parliament, we fhall find no men-
tion of any new Ally except the *Spaniard*, whofe Affairs at that
time, through the Defects of his own Government, and the
Treachery of our Minifters,were reduced to fo defperate a State,
that he might well be a Burden to us ; but there was little to be
hoped from a Friendfhip with him, unlefs by the name of a
League, to recommend our Minifters to a new Parliament, and
cozen Country Gentlemen out of their Money. But upon
perufal of that League, it appears by the Third, Fourth and
Fifth Articles, that it was like to create us Trouble enough ; for
it engages us indefinitely to enter into all the Quarrels of the
Spaniards, though they happened in the *Weft Indies*, or the *Phi-
lipine Iflands*, or were drawn upon himfelf by his own Injuftice
or caufelefs Provocations. By this we fhall be obliged to efpoufe
his difference with the Duke of *Brandenburgh*, though all that
Duke did, was according to the Law of Nations, to Reprize
Spanifh Ships for a juft Debt frequently demanded in vain. By
this we fhall be obliged to engage in his prefent War with the
Portuguefe, though he by his violent feizing of the Ifland of St.
Gabriel, which had long been in their peaceable poffeffion,
without once demanding it of them, has moft juftly provoked
the *Portuguefe* to invade *Spain*. Nor are we bound only to
affift him in cafe of an Invafion ; but in cafe of any Difturbance
whatfoever, which muft be intended of inteftine Troubles,
(and it is fo directly explained in the fecret Article, which all
Europe fays was figned at the fame time.) So that if the prefent
King of *Spain* fhould imitate his Great Grandfather, *Philip* the
Second,and opprefs any of his Subjects,as cruelly as he did thofe
of the *Low Countries*, and fo force them to a neceffary Self-De-
fence , we have renounced the policy of our Anceftors, who
thought it their Intereft as well as their Duty to fuccor the di-
ftreffed, and muft not only aid him with 8000 Men for three
Months, to make thofe People Slaves, but if the matter cannot
be

(13)

be compofed in that time, make War upon them, with our whole Force both by Land and Sea. But that which concerns us yet nearer in this League, is, that this Obligation of affiftance was mutual, fo that if a Difturbance fhould happen hereafter in *England,* upon any attempt to change our Religion or our Government, though it was in the time of his Majefties Succeffors, the Moft Catholick King is obliged by this League, (which we are ftill to believe was entred into, for the fecurity of the Proteftant Religion,and the good of the Nation) to give Aid to fo Pious a Defign, and to make War upon the People with all his Forces both by Land and Sea. And therefore it was no wonder that the Minifters were not forward in fhewing this League to the Parliament, who would foon have obferved all thefe Inconveniences, and have feen how little fuch a League could contribute to the preferving the General Peace, or to the Securing of *Flanders,* fince the *French* King may within one months time poffefs himfelf of it, and we by the League are not obliged to fend our Succors till Three Months after the Invafion. So that they would upon the whole matter, have been inclined to fufpect, that the main End of this League was only to ferve for a handfom pretence to raife an Army in *England,*and if the people here fhould grow difcontented at it,and any little Diforders fhould enfue, the *Spaniard* is thereby obliged to fend over Forces to fupprefs them.

The next thing *recommended to them, was the farther Examination of the Plot,* and every one who has obferved what has paffed for more than two years together, cannot doubt that this was fincerely defired by fuch as are moft in Credit with his Majefty ; and then furely the Parliament deferved not to be cenfured upon this Account, fince the Examination of fo many new Witneffes, the Tryal of the Lord *Stafford,*the great Preparations for the Tryals of the reft of the Lords,and their diligent Enquiry into the Horrid *Irifh* Treafons, fhew that the Parliament wanted no Diligence to purfue his Majefties good Intentions in that Affair.

And when His *Majefty defired from the Parliament their Advice and Affiftance concerning the Prefervation of* Tangier ; the Commons did not neglect to give it its due Confideration. They truly reprefented to Him how that important place came to be brought into *fuch Exigencies, after fo vaft a Treafure expended*

Addrefs prefentid 21 Dec, 1680. Addrefs prefented 29 Nov. 1680.

to

to make it useful ; and that nothing better could be expected of a Town, *for the moſt part put under Popiſh Governors*, and always fill'd with a *Popiſh Gariſon*.   Theſe were Evils in his Majeſty's own Power to redreſs, and they *adviſed him to it* ; nor did they reſt there, but promiſe to aſſiſt him in defence of it, as ſoon as ever they could be reaſonably ſecured, that any Supply which they gave for that purpoſe, ſhould not be uſed *to augment the Strength of our Popiſh Adverſaries, and to encreaſe our Dangers at Home.* They had more than once ſeen Mony employed directly contrary to the end for which it was given by Parliament, and they had too great cauſe of Fear it might be ſo again ; and they knew that ſuch a Miſimployment would have been fatal at that Time.   But above all, they conſidered the imminent Danger which threatned them with certain Ruin at Home, and therefore juſtly thought that to leave the Conſideration of *England* to provide for *Tangier*, would be to act like a Man that ſhould ſend his Servants to mend a Gap in his Hedg when he ſaw his Houſe on Fire, and his Family like to be conſumed in it.

We are next told, that His *Majeſty offered to concur in any Remedies that could be propoſed for the Security of the Proteſtant Religion* ; and we muſt own that he did indeed make ſuch an *Offer* ; but he was pleaſed to go no farther, for thoſe Remedies which the Commons tendered were rejected, and thoſe which they were preparing, were prevented by a Diſſolution.   •

We have ſeen the great Things which the King did on his part ; let us now reflect on thoſe Inſtances which are ſingled out as ſo many *unſuitable Returns of the Commons*. They are complained of for preſenting *Addreſſes in the nature of Remonſtrances rather than Anſwers.* Under what unhappy Circumſtances do we find our ſelves, when our Repreſentatives can never behave themſelves with that Caution, but they will be miſ-interpreted at Court ? If the Commons had return'd Anſwer to his Majeſty's Meſſages, without ſhewing upon what Grounds they proceeded, they had then been accuſed as Men acting peremptorily, and without reaſon ; if they modeſtly expreſs the Reaſons of their Reſolutions, they are then ſaid to Remonſtrate. But what the Miniſters would have this word Remonſtrance ſignify, what Crime it is they mean thereby, to charge the Commons with, is unknown to an *Engliſh* Reader. Perhaps they who are better acquainted with *French*-men, know ſome pernicious thing
which

which it imports. If they mean by a Remonſtrance, a *declaring the Cauſes and Reaſons* of what they do, it will not ſurely be imputed as a Fault in them, ſince 'tis a way of proceeding which His Majeſties Miniſters have juſtified by their own Example, having in His Majeſties Name vouchſafed to *declare the Cauſes and Reaſons of his Actions* to his People.

But the Commons made *Arbitrary Orders for taking Perſons into Cuſtody, for matters that had no Relation to Priviledges of Parliament*. The Contrivers of this Declaration, who are ſo particular in other things, would have done well to have given ſome inſtances of theſe Orders.

If they intend by theſe General Words, to reflect on the Orders made to take thoſe degenerate Wretches into Cuſtody, who publiſhed under their Hands their Abhorrence of Parliaments, and of thoſe who in an humble and lawful manner Petitioned for their Sitting, in a time of ſuch extream neceſſity. Surely they are not in good earneſt, they cannot believe themſelves, when they ſay, that *theſe Matters* had no *Relation to Priviledges of Parliament*. If the Priviledge of Parliament be concern'd when an injury is done to any particular Member, how much more is it touched when Men ſtrike at Parliaments themſelves, and endeavour to wound the very Conſtitution? If this be ſaid with Relation to *Sheridon*, who has ſince troubled the World with ſo many idle impudent Pamphlets upon that account, 'tis plain that his Commitment was only in order to examine him about the Popiſh Plot, and his Endeavors to ſtifle it, (though his contemptuous Behaviour to the Houſe, deſerved a much longer Confinement) and 'twas Inſolence in him to Arraign their Juſtice, becauſe they did not inſtantly leave all their great Debates to diſpatch the buſineſs relating to him.

Thompſon of *Briſtol*, was Guilty of divers great Breaches of Priviledge ; but yet his Commitment was only in order to an Impeachment; and as ſoon as they had gone through with his Examination, they ordered him to be ſet at Liberty, giving Security to anſwer the Impeachment which they had voted againſt him. But is it a thing ſo ſtrange and new to the Authors of the Declaration, that the Houſe of Commons ſhould Order Men to be taken into Cuſtody for matters not relating to Priviledg? Have they not heard, that in the 4 *Edw.* 6. *Cricketoſt* was Committed for Confedertaing in an Eſcape ; that 18 *Jac.*

Sir

Sir *Francis Mitchel* was Comitted for Mifdemeanors, in pro-
curing a Patent for the Forfeitures of Recognizances, together
with *Fowles Gerrard*, and divers others, (none of which were
Members of Parliament) that 20 *Jac.* Dr. *Harris* was taken
into Cuftody for misbehaving himfelf in Preaching ; and that
3 *Car. Burgeffe* was Committed for Faults in Catechizing, and
Levet for prefuming to exercife a Patent, which had been adjudged a Grievance by a Committee of the Commons in a former Parliament.

There would be no end of giving Inftances of thofe Commit-
ments, which may be obferved in almoft every Parliament, fo
that the Houfe of Commons did but tread in the Steps of their
Predeceffors, and thefe forts of Orders were not new, though
the Declaration takes the Liberty to call them Arbitrary. The
Commons had betrayed their Truft, if they had not afferted the
Right of Petitioning, which had been juft before fhaken by fuch
a *ftrange Illegal and Arbitrary Proclamation.*

But now we come to the Tranfcendent monftrous Crimes,
which can never be forgiven by the Minifters, the giving them
their due Character, which every Man of Underftanding had
fix'd upon them long before : the whole Current of their Counfels being a full Proof of the Truth of the Charge. But what
colour is there for calling thefe Votes illegal ? *Is it* illegal for
the Commons to impeach perfons, whom they have good reafon to judg Enemies to the King and Kingdom ? *Is it* Illegal to
determin by a Vote (which is the only way of finding the
Sence of the Houfe) who are Wicked Counfellors, and deferve
to be impeach'd ? Could the Commons have called the Parties
accufed to make their Anfwer before themfelves ? Had they not
a proper time for their Defence when they came to their Tryals ?
and might they not have cleared their Innocence much better, if
they durft have put that in Iffue) by a Tryal, than a Diffolution
of the Parliament ? But fhould we grant that thefe Votes were
not made in Order to an Impeachment, yet ftill there is nothing
Illegal, nothing extraordinary in them. For the Commons in
Parliament, have ever ufed two ways in delivering their Country
from pernicious and powerful Favorites, the one is in a Parliamentary Courfe of Juftice by Impeaching them, which is ufed
when they judg it needful to make them publick Examples, by
Capital, or other high Punifhments, for the terror of others :
The

The other is by immediate Addreſs to the King to remove them as unfaithful or unprofitable Servants. Their Lives their Liberties or Eſtates are never endangered, but when they are proceeded againſt in the former of theſe ways. Then legal evidence of their Guilt is neceſſary, then there muſt be a proper time allowed for their defence. In the other way the Parliament act as the Kings great Council, and when either Houſe obſerve that Affairs are ill adminiſtred, that the advice of Parliaments is rejected or ſlighted, the Courſe of Juſtice perverted, our Councels betray'd, Grievances multiplyed, and the Government weakly and diſorderly managed, (of all which our Laws have made it impoſſible for the King to be guilty). They neceſſarily muſt, and always have charg'd thoſe who had the Adminiſtration of Affairs, and the Kings Ear, as the Authors of theſe miſchiefs, and have from time to time applyed themſelves to him by Addreſſes for their Removal from his Preſence and Councils. There be many things plain and evident beyond the Teſtimony of any Witneſſes, which yet can never be proved in a legal way. If the King will hearken to none but two or three of his Minions, muſt we not conclude that every thing that is done comes from their Advice? And yet, if this way of repreſenting things to the King were not allowed, they might eaſily fruſtrate the enquiries of a Parliament. It is but to whiſper their Counſels, and they are ſafe. The Parliament may be buſied in ſuch great Affairs, as will not ſuffer them to purſue every Offender through a long Proceſs; and beſides there may be many reaſons why a man ſhould be turn'd out of a ſervice, which perhaps would not extend to ſubject him to puniſhment. The People themſelves are highly concern'd in the great Officers and Miniſters of State, who are Servants to the Kingdom as well as to the King. And the Repreſentatives of the People, the Commons, whoſe buſineſs it is to preſent all Grievances, as they are moſt likely to obſerve ſooneſt the Folly and Treachery of thoſe publick Servants, (the greateſt of all Grievances) ſo this Repreſentation ought to have no little weight with the Prince. This was underſtood ſo well by *H. 4.* a wiſe and brave Prince, that when the Commons complain'd againſt four of his Servants, and Councellors, deſiring they might be removed, he came into Parliament and there declared openly that though he knew nothing againſt them in particular, yet he was

Rot. Parl. 5 H. 4. Nu. 5.

C   aſſured

affured that what the Lords and Commons defired of him, was for the good of himfelf and his Kingdom; and therefore he did comply with them, and banifh'd thofe four Perfons from his Prefence and Councils, declaring at the fame time, that he would do fo by any others who fhould be near His Royal Perfon, if they were fo unhappy to fall under the Hatred and Indignation of his People. The Records and Hiftories of the Reigns of *Edward* the firft, *Edw*. II. *Edw*. III. and indeed of all other fucceeding Kings are full of fuch Addreffes as thefe; but no Hiftory or Record can fhew that ever they were called illegal or Un-Parliamentary till now.

Then the Minifters durft not appeal to the People againft their own Reprefentatives, but ours at prefent have either got fome new Law in the point, or have attained to a greater degree of Confidence, then any that went before them. The beft of our Princes have with thanks acknowledged the Care and Duty of their Parliaments, in telling them of the Corruption and Folly of their Favourites. *Ed*. I. *Ed*. III. *Hen*. V. and *Q. El*. never fail'd to do it, and no Names are remembred with greater Honour in the Englifh Annals. Whilft the diforderly, the Troublefome and Unfortunate Reigns of *H*. III. *Ed*. II. *R*. II. and *H*. the VI. ought to ferve as Land-marks to warn fucceeding Kings from preferring fecret Councels to the Wifdom of their Parliaments.

But none of the Proceedings of the Houfe of Commons, have been more cenfured at Court, and with lefs Juftice, than their Vote about the Anticipation of feveral Branches of the Revenue. An objection which could proceed from nothing, but a total ignorance of the Nature of Publick Treafure in our own, and all other Nations, which was ever efteem'd Sacred & Un-alienable. All the Acts of refumption in the times of *H*. IV. *H*. VI. and other of our Kings were founded upon this Maxim, otherwife there could not be conceived any groffer injuftice, than to declare Alienations to be void, which Kings had lawful power to make. It was upon this Maxim that the Parliament declar'd the Grant to the Pope of the yearly fum of 1000 marks, wherewith K. *John* had charg'd the Inheritance of the Crown, to be Null. It was for this caufe that in the year 1670. His Majefty procured, an Act of Parliament, to enable him to fell the Fee Farm Rents, and it is the beft excufe that can be made

for

for thofe Minifters who in the year 1672. advifed the poft-
poning of all payments to the Bankers out of the Exchequer,
that they judged all fecurities by way of Anticipation of the
Revenue, illegal and void in themfelves.

Refumptions have been frequent in every Kingdom, the
King of *Sweden* within thefe few Months, has, by the Advice
of the States, refumed all the Lands which His Predeceffors had
in many years before granted from the Crown. No Country
did ever believe the Prince, how abfolute foever in other
things, had power to fell or give away the Revenue of the
Kingdom, and leave his Succeffor a Beggar. All thofe Acts of
the Roman Emperors, whereby they wafted the Treafure of
the Empire, were refcinded by their Succeffors ; and *Tacitus*
obferves, that the firft of them that look't upon the publick
Treafure as his own, was *Claudius* the weakeft and moft fot-
tifh of them all. The prefent King of *France* did within thefe
twelve years, by the confent of his feveral Parliaments, refume
all the Demefnes of the Crown which had been Granted away
by himfelf or his Predeceffors. That haughty Monarch, as
much power as he pretends to, not being afham'd to own that
he wanted power to make fuch Alienations,and that Kings had
that happy inability, that they could do nothing contrary to *Traitte*
the Laws of their Countrey. This notion feems founded in the *des dro-*
reafon of mankind,fince Barbarifm it felf cannot efface it. The *its de la*
Ottoman Emperors difpofe Arbitrarily of the Lives and Eftates *Ont cette*
of their Subjects, but yet they efteem it the moft deteftable *bien heu-*
wickednefs, to employ the Tributes and Growing Revenues *reufe im-*
of the Provinces,(which they call the Sacred blood of the Peo- *puiffance*
ple;) upon any other than publick occafions. And our Kings *vir rien*
H. IV. and *H.*VII,underftood fo well the different power they *faire con-*
had in ufing their private Inheritances and thofe of the Crown, *tre les*
that they took care,by Authority of Parliament,to feparate the *Loys de*
Dutchy of *Lancafter* from the Crown, and to keep the defcent *leur Pais.*
of it diftinct. But our prefent Courtiers are quite of another *de Rebus*
Opinion, who fpeak of the Revenue of the Crown as if *Turcicis.*
it were a private Patrimony, and defign'd only for domeftick
ufes, and for the Pleafures of the Prince.

The Revenues of the Crown of *England* are in their own nature appropriated to Publick Service, & therefore cannot without injuftice be diverted or Anticipated. For either the Publick

Reve-

Revenue is fufficient to anfwer the neceffary Occafions of the Government, and then there is no colour for Anticipations, or elfe by fome extraordinary accident the K. is reduced to want an extraordinary fupply, and then he ought to refort to his Parliament. Thus wifely did our Anceftors provide, that the K. and His People fhould have frequent need of one another, and by having frequent opportunities of mutually relieving one anothers wants, be fure ever to preferve a dutiful affection in the Subject, and a fartherly tendernefs in the Prince. When the King had occafion for the Liberality of his People, he would be well inclin'd to hear and redrefs their Grievances, and when they wanted eafe from Oppreffions they would not fail with alacrity to fupply the occafions of the Crown. And therefore it has ever been efteem'd a crime in Counfellors who perfwaded the King to Anticipate his Revenue, and a Crime in thofe who furnifht Money upon fuch Anticipations in an Extraordinary way, however extraordinary the Occafion might be. For this caufe it was that the Parliament in the 35th. of H. 8. did not only difcharge all thofe debts which the K. had contracted, but enacted that thofe Lenders who had been before paid again by the King, fhould refund all thofe fums into the Exchequer, as Judging it a reafonable punifhment, to make them forfeit the Money they lent, fince they had gone about to introduce fo dangerous a Precedent.

The true way to put the King out of a *poffibility of fupporting the Government*, is to let him waft in one year that Money, which ought to bear the charge of the Government for feven. This is the direct method to deftroy the *Credit of the Crown both Abroad and at Home*. If the King refolve never to pay the Money which he Borrows, what Faith will be given to Royal Promifes, and the Honour of the Nation will fuffer in that of the Prince, & if it muft be put upon the People to repay it, this would be a way to impofe a neceffity of giving Taxes without end, whether they would or no. And therefore (as Mercenary as they were) the Penfioners would never difcharge the Revenue of the Anticipations to the Bankers. Now the Commons having the inconvenience of this before their Eyes in fo frefh an inftance, and having their Ears fill'd with the daily cries of fo many Widows and Orphans; were obliged in duty to give a Public Caution to the People, that they fhould not run agan into

the

the fame Error. Not only becaufe they judged all Securities
of that kind abfolutely void, but becaufe they knew no future
Parliament could without breach of Truft repay that Money
which was at firft borrowed only to prevent the Sitting of a
Parliament, and which could never be paid without Counte-
nancing a Method fo deftructive to our Conftitution. Nor have
former Parliaments been lefs careful and nice in giving the leaft
allowance to any unufual ways of taking up Money, without
common Confent, having fo very often declar'd, *that the King
cannot fupply his moft preffing Neceffities , either by Loans, or
by the Benevolence of his Subjects , which by the exprefs words* 1 R. 3.
of the Statute , are damned and annulled for ever. But the ᶜᵃᵖ. 2.
Houfe of Commons were fo cautious of giving any juft occafion of Cavil, that they reftrain'd their Votes much more
than they needed to have done: For they extended them only
to three Branches of the Revenue, all which were by feveral
Acts of Parliament given to his prefent Majefty. And furely
every one will agree, that when the King receives a Gift from
his People, he takes it under fuch Conditions, and ought to imploy it in fuch a manner, and for fuch purpofes as they direct.
We muft therefore confult the feveral Acts by which thofe
Branches were fetled ; if we would judge rightly whether the
Commons had not particular Reafons for what they did. The
Statute 12 Car. 2. c. 4. fays, That *the Commons repofing Truft* 12 Car.
in his Majefty for guarding the Seas againft all Perfons intend- c. 4. 4.
ing the Difturbance of Trade , and the invading of the Realm, to firm'd
that intent do give him the Tonnage and Poundage, &c. This is as Car. c.
direct an Appropriation as Words can make, and therefore
as it is manifeft wrong to the Subject, to divert any part of this
Branch to other ufes ; fo for the King to anticipate it, is plainly to difable himfelf to perform *the Truft repofed in Him.* And
the late long Parliament thought this matter fo clear, that
about two years before their Diffolution, they paffed a Vote,
with Relation to the Cuftoms, in almoft the fame Words. 12 Car.
The Parliament which gave the Excife were fo far from c. 23. a
thinking that the King had power to charge or difpofe of it
as his own, that by a fpecial Claufe in the Act, whereby they
give it, they were careful to *impower him to difpofe of it, or any part
of it by way of Farm*, and to Enact *that fuch Contracts fhall be effectual in Law; fo as they be not for a longer time than three years.* The

Act

Act, whereby the Hearth-money was given, declares that it was done to the end, *that the publick Revenue might be proportioned to the publick Charge* ; and 'tis impoffible that fhould ever be, whilft it is liable to be pre-ingaged and anticipated. And the Parliament were fo careful to preferve this Tax always clear and uncharg'd, that they made it penal for any one fo much as *to accept of any Penfion or Grant for years, or any other Eftate, or any Summ of Money out of the Revenue arifing by vertue of that Act, from the King, his Heirs or Succeffors.* Surely if the Penners of this Declaration had not been altogether ignorant of our own Laws, and of the Policy of all other Countries and Ages, they would never have printed thofe Votes, in hopes thereby to have expofed the Commons to the World. They would not have had the face to fay, that thereby the *King was expofed to Danger, deprived of a poffibility of fupporting the Government,* and *reduc'd to a more helplefs Condition than the meaneft of His Subjects.* This we are fure of, that the inviolable obferving of thefe Statutes, will be fo far from reducing His Majefty to a more helplefs Condition than the meaneft of his Subjects, that it will ftill leave him in a better condition than the richeft and greateft of his Anceftors, none of which were ever Mafters of fuch a Revenue.

The H. of Commons are in the next place accufed of a very high Crime, the affuming to themfelves a power of fufpending Acts of Parliament, becaufe they declared that it was their opinion, *That the Profecution of Proteftant Diffenters upon the Penal Laws, is at this time grievous to the Subject, a weakning of the Proteftant Intereft, an Incouragement to Popery, and dangerous to the Peace of the Kingdom.* The Minifters remembred that not many years ago, the whole Nation was juftly alarm'd upon the affuming an Arbitrary Power of fufpending Penal Laws, and therefore they thought it would be very popular to accufe the Commons of fuch an attempt. But how they could poffible mifinterpret a Vote at that rate, how they could fay the Commons pretended to a Power of repealing Laws, when they only declare their Opinion of the inconveniency of them, will never be underftood till the Authors of this are pleafed to *fhew their Caufes and Reafons* for it in a fecond *Declaration.* Every impartial man will own, that the Commons had reafon for this Opinion of theirs. They had with great anxiety obferved

ferved that the prefent defign of the Papifts was not againft any
one fort of Proteftants, but univerfal, and for extirpating the
Reform'd Religion. They faw what advantages thefe Enemies
made of our Divifions, and how cunningly they diverted us from
profecuting them, by fomenting our jealoufies of one another.
They faw the ftrength and nearnefs of the King of *France*, and
judged of his Inclinations by his ufage of his own Proteftant
Subjects. They confider'd the number, and the bloody Principles
of the *Irifh*, and what Confpiracies were form'd there, and even
ripe for Execution; and that *Scotland* was already delivered into the hands of a Prince, the known head of the Papifts in thefe
Kingdoms, and the occafion of all their Plots and Infolencies,
as more than one Parliament had declared. They could not
but take notice into what hands the moft confiderable Trufts
both Civil and Military were put, and that notwithftanding all
Addreffes, and all Proclamations for a ftrict Execution of the
Penal Laws againft Papifts, yet their Faction fo far prevailed,
that they were eluded, and only the diffenting Proteftants
fmarted under the edge of them. In the midft of fuch Circumftances was there not caufe to think an Union of all Proteftants
neceffary, and could they have any juft ground to believe that
the Diffenters, whilft they lay under the Preffures of fevere
Laws, fhould with fuch Alacrity and Courage as was requifite,
undertake the defence of a Country where they were fo ill treat-
ed? A long and fad Experience had fhew'd how vain the
Endeavours of former Parliaments had been to force us to be
all of one Opinion, and therefore the Houfe of Commons re-
folv'd to take a fure way to make us of one Affection. They
knew that fome bufie men would be ftriking whilft there were
Weapons at hand; and therefore to make us live at peace, they
meant to take away all occafions of provoking, or being provoked. In order to a general Repeal of thefe Laws, they firft
came to a Vote declaring the neceffity of it, to which there was
not one Negative in the Houfe : A Vote of this nature does for
the moft part precede the bringing in of a Bill for the Repeal
of any General Law. And it had been a great prefumption in a
particular Member to have asked leave to have brought in a
Bill for repealing fo many Laws, together, till the Houfe had
firft declar'd, that in their opinion they were *grievous and incon-
venient*. No *Englifh man* could be fo ignorant of our Laws, none
but

but a *French-man* could have confidence to declaim againſt a proceeding ſo regular and Parliamentary as this. Where was the *diſregard to the Laws Eſtabliſhed*, for the Commons to attempt the abrogating of a Law that is *grievous to the Subject, and dangerous to the Peace of the Kingdom?* Is it *a ſuſpending Acts of Parliament*, if they declare a Law to be *grievous and dangerous* in their *Opinion*, before they ſet about the Repeal of it? And is there any ground to doubt but that a Bill would have paſs'd that Houſe, purſuant to this Vote, had it not been prevented by a Diſſolution? Nor was there the leaſt direction or ſignification to *the Judges*, which might give any occaſion for the Reflection which follows in the Declaration. The due and impartial Execution of the Laws, is the unqueſtionable Duty of the Judges, and we hope they will always remember that duty ſo well, as not to neceſſitate a H. of Commons to do theirs, by calling them to account for making private Inſtructions the Rule of their Judgments, and acting as men who have more regard to their Places than their Oaths. 'Tis too well known who it is that ſollicites and manages in favour of Judges, when a H. of Commons does demand Juſtice againſt them, for breaking their Oaths. And therefore the Publiſhers of this Declaration had ſaid ſomething well, if when they tell us the Judges ought not to break their Oaths in Reverence to the Votes of either H. they had been pleaſed to add, not in reſpect of any Command from the K. or Favorites. Then we ſhould have no more Letters from Secretaries of State to Judges ſitting upon the Bench. Then we ſhould have no more Proclamations like that of the 14th Oct. 1662. forbidding the Execution of the Laws concerning Highways. Nor that of the 10th of *May*, 1672. diſpenſing with divers Clauſes in the Acts of Parliament for increaſe of Shipping. Nor any more Declarations like that of the 15. of *March*, 1672. ſuſpending the Penal Laws in matters Eccleſiaſtical.

But the Judges are ſworn to execute all Laws, yet there is no obligation upon any man to inform againſt another. And therefore though the Miniſters prevented the Repeal of thoſe Laws, 'tis to be hop'd that this Vote will reſtrain every Engliſhman from proſecuting Proteſtants, when ſo wiſe and great a body have declared the pernicious effects of ſuch a Proſecution. 'Tis moſt true, that in *England* no Law is abrogated by deſuetude, but it is no leſs true, that there are many Laws ſtill unre-
pealed

peal'd which are never Executed, nor can be without publick
detriment. The Judges know of many fuch dormant Laws,
and yet they do not quicken the People to put them in Execution, nor think themfelves Guilty of Perjury that they do not:
fuch are the Laws for wearing Caps, for keeping Lent, thofe
concerning Bowes and Arrows, about killing Calves, ard
Lambs, and many others. And thofe who vex men by Infor-
mation on fuch antiquated Laws, have been ever lookt upon as
Infamous, and Difturbers of the publick quiet. Hence it is that
there are no Names remembred with greater deteftation than
thofe of *Empfon* and *Dudley*, the whole Kingdom abhorr'd them
as Monfters in the time of *H.* VII. and they were punifh'd as
Traitors in the Reign of his Son.

The alteration of the circumftances whereupon a Law was
made, or if it be againft the genius of the People, or have
effects contrary to the intent of the Makers, will foon caufe any
Law to be difufed, and after a little difufe, the reviving of it
will be thought Oppreffion. Efpecially if experience has fhewn,
that by the non-execution, the quiet, the fafety, and Trade of
the Nation have been promoted ; of all which the Commons,
who are fent from every part of the Kingdom, are able to make
the cleareft Judgment. Therefore after they have declared
their Opinions of the Inconvenience of reviving the Execution
of thefe Laws, which have lain afleep for divers years, tho' the
Judges muft proceed, if any forward Informers fhould give
them the trouble, yet they would not act wifely or honeftly if
they fhould Encourage Informers, or quicken Juries by ftrict
and fevere charges. Efpecially if it be confidered, that the Lords
alfo were preparing Bills in favor of Diffenters, and that the
King has wifh'd often it was in his power to eafe them. So that
tho' there be no Act of Repeal formerly paffed, we have the
confent and defire of all who have any fhare in making Acts.
But let this Vote have what confequence it will, yet fure the
Minifters had forgot that the Black Rod was at the door of the
Houfe, to require them to attend His Majefty at the very time
when it was made, otherwife they would not have numbred it
amongft the caufes *which occafioned the King to part with that
Parliament.* And thofe that knew His Majefty was putting on
his Robes before that Vote paffed, might imagine a Diffolution thus forefeen, might occafion it, but cannot be brought to

believe

believe, that the Vote which was not in being, could occasion the Diffolution. Thefe are the *proceedings* which the Minifters judg *unwarrantable* in the Parliament at *Weftminfter*, and for which they prevailed with His Majefty *to part with it.* But fince it is evident upon Examination, that the principles of our Conftitution, the method of Parliaments, and the precedents of every Age, were their Guide and Warrant in all thofe things; furely the K. muft needs be alike offended with the Men about him, for perfwading him to Diffolve that Parliament without any caufe; and for fetting forth in his Name a Declaration of fuch pretended caufe as every man almoft fees through, and contrived only to cover thofe Reafons which they durft not own. But with what face can they objeƈ to the Houfe of Commons their *ftrange Illegal Votes declaring divers Eminent Perfens to be Enemies to the King and Kingdom,* when at the fame time they arrogate to themfelves an unheard of Authority to Arraign one of the three Eftates in the face of the World, for *ufurping power over the Laws, Imprifoning their fellow Subjeƈs Arbitrarily, expofing the Kingdom to the greateft dangers, and endeavouring to deprive the King of all poffibility of fupporting the Government,* and all this without any order or procefs of Law, without hearing of their defence, and as much without any reafon, as Precedent. We have had Minifters heretofore fo bold, (yet ever with ill fuccefs) as to accufe a pretended Faƈtious party in the Houfe, but never did any go fo high as openly to Reprefent the whole H. of Commons as a Faƈtion, much lefs, to caufe them to be denounced in all the Churches of the Kingdom, that fo the People might look upon it as a kind of Excommunication. But if they erred in the things they judged rightly in the choice of the Perfons who were to publifh it. Blind Obedience was requifite, where fuch unjuftifiable things were impofed, and that could be no where fo entire, as amongft thofe Clergy-men whofe preferment depended upon it. Therefore it was ordered that this Declaration fhould be read by them, being pretty well affured that they would not unwillingly read in the Desk, a Paper fo fuitable to the Doƈtrin wᶜʰ fome of them had often declared in the Pulpit. It did not become them to enquire whether they had fufficient Authority for what they did; fince the Printer called it the K's. Declaration, & whether they might not one day be call'd to account for publifhing it; nor once to ask if

what

what His Majefty fingly ordered when he fate in Council, and came forth without the ftamp of the great Seal, gave them a fufficient warrant to read it publickly.

Clergy-men feldom make Reflections of this kind, leaft they fhould be thought to difpute the commands of their Superiors. It hath been obferved, that they who allow unto themfelves the liberty of doubting, advance their fortunes very flowly, whilft fuch who obey without fcruple, go on with a fuccefs equal to their ambition. And this carries them on without fear or fhame, and as little thought of a Parliament, as the Court Favourites who took care to Diffolve that at *Oxford*, before they durft tell us the faults of that at *Weftminfter*.

We have already anfwer'd the mifcarriages objected to the firft, and may now take a view of thofe imputed to the other, which they fay *was Affembled as foon as that was Diffolved*, and might have added *Diffolved as foon as Affembled*. The Minifters having imploy'd the People forty days in chufing Knights and Burgeffes, to be fent home in eight, with a Declaration after them, as if they had been called together only to be affronted. The Declaration doth not tell us of any gracious expreffions ufed at the opening of that Parliament, perhaps becaufe the ftore was exhaufted by the abundance which His Majefty was pleafed to beftow on them in his former Speeches. But we ought to believe that His Majefties Heart was as full of them as ever, and if he did not exprefs them, it is to be imputed unto the Minifters, who diverted him from his own inclinations, and brought him to ufe a language until that day unknown unto Parliaments. The Gracious Speech then made, and the Gracious Declaration that followed, are fo much of a piece, that we may juftly conclude the fame Perfons to have been Authors of both. However His Majefty failed not to give good advice unto them, who were called together to advife him. The Parliament had fo much refpect for their K: as not particulirly to complain of the great invafion, that was made upon their liberty of propofing and debating Laws, by his telling them before hand what things they fhould meddle with, and what things, no reafons they could offer, fhould perfwade him to confent unto.

But every man muft be moved to hear it charged upon them as an unpardonable difobedience, that they did not obfequioufly fubmit to that irregular Command, of not touching on the bu-

finefs

finefs of the Succeffion. Shall two or three unknown Minions take upon them, like the Lords of the Articles of *Scotland*, to preferibe unto an Englifh Parliament what things they fhall treat of? Do they intend to have Parliaments *inter inftrumenta fervitutis*, as the Romans had Kings in our Country? This would quickly be, if what was then attempted had fucceeded, and fhould be fo purfued hereafter, that Parliaments fhould be directed what they were to meddle with, and threatned if they do any other thing. For the lofs of Freedom of debate in Parliament, will foon and certainly be followed by a general lofs of Liberty. Without failing in the refpect which all good Subjects owe unto the King, it may be faid, that His Majefty ought to diveft himfelf of all private inclinations, and force his own Affections to yield unto the publick concernments: And therefore His Parliaments ought to inform him impartially, of that which tends to the good of thofe they reprefent, without regard of perfonal paffions, and might worthily be blam'd, if they did not believe, that he would forgo them all for the fafety of his people. Therefore if in it felf it was lawful to propofe a Bill for excluding the Duke of *York* from the Crown, the doing it after fuch an unwarrantable fignification of his pleafure would not make it otherwife. And the unufual ftiffnefs which the King hath fhown upon this occafion, begins to be fufpected not to proceed from any fondnefs to the Perfon of his Brother, much lefs from any thought of danger to the Englifh Monarchy by fuch a Law, but from the influence of fome few ill men upon his Royal Mind, who being Creatures to the Duke, or Penfioners to *France*, are reftlefs to prevent a good underftanding between the King and his people; juftly fearing, that if ever he comes to have a true fence of their affections to him, he would deliver up to Juftice thefe wicked wretches, who have infected him with the fatal notion, That the interefts of his people are not only diftinct, but oppofite to his.

His Majefty does not feem to doubt of his power in conjunction with his Parliament, to exclude his Brother. He very well know's this power hath been often exerted in the time of his Predeceffors. But the reafon given for his refufal to comply with the interefts and defires of his Subjects, is, becaufe it was a *point which concerned him fo near in Honour, Juftice and Confcience.* Is it not honourable for a Prince, to be True and

Faith-

Faithful to his Word and Oath ? to keep and maintain the Religion and Laws eftablifhed ? Nay, can it be thought difhonourable unto him,to love the fafety and welfare of his People, and the true Religion eftablifhed among them, above the temporal Glory and Greatnefs of his perfonal Relations ? Is it not juft, in conjunction with his Parliament, for his Peoples fafety, to make ufe of a power warranted by our *Englifh* Laws, and the Examples of former Ages ? Or is it juft for the Father of his Country to expofe all his Children to ruin, out of fondnefs unto a Brother ? May it not rather be thought unjuft to abandon the Religion, Laws and Liberties of his People, which he is fworn to maintain and defend, and expofe them to the Ambition and Rage of one that thinks himfelf bound in Confcience to fubvert them ? If his Majefty is pleafed to remember what Religion the Duke profeffeth, can he think himfelf obliged in *Confcience* to fuffer him to afcend the Throne, who will certainly endeavour to overthrow the eftablifhed Religion, and fet up the worft of Superftitions and Idolatry in the room of it ? Or if it be true, that all obligations of Honour, Juftice and Confcience, are comprehended in a grateful return of fuch benefits as have been received, can his Majefty believe that he doth duly repay unto his Proteftant Subjects the kindnefs they fhewed him, when they recalled him from a miferable helplefs banifhment, and with fo much dutiful affection placed him in the Throne, enlarged his Rvenue above what any of his Predeceffors had enjoyed,& gave him vafter Sums of Money in twenty years, than had been beftowed upon all the Kings fince *William* the *firft*; fhould he after all this deliver them up to be ruin'd by his Brother ? It cannot be faid that he had therein more regard unto the Government than to the Perfon, feeing it is evident the Bill of Exclufion had no ways prejudiced the legal Monarchy,which his Majefty doth now enjoy with all the Rights and Powers which his wife and brave Anceftors did ever claim, becaufe many Acts of the like nature have paffed heretofore upon lefs neceffary occafions.

The prefervation of every Government depends upon an exact adherence unto its Principles,and the effential Principle of the *Englifh* Monarchy, being that well proportioned diftribution of Powers, whereby the Law doth at once provide for the greatnefs of the King,and the fafety of the People,the Government can fubfift no longer, than whilft the Monarch enjoying

the

(30)

the Power which the Law doth give him, is enabled to perform the part it allows unto him, and the People are duly protected in their Rights and Liberties. For this reason our Ancestors have been always more careful to preserve the Government inviolable, than to favour any personal Pretences, and have therein conformed themselves to the practice of all other Nations, whose examples deserve to be followed. Nay, we know of none so slavishly addicted unto any Person or Family, as for any reason whatsoever, to admit of a Prince who openly professed a Religion contrary to that which was established amongst them. It were easie to alledge multitude of Examples of those who have rejected Princes for reasons of far less weight than difference in Religion, as *Robert* of *Normandy*, *Charles* of *Lorrain*, *Alphonso a Desperadado* of *Spain*; but those of a latter date, against whom there was no other exception than for their Religion, suteth better with our occasion. Among whom it is needless to name *Henry* of *Bourbon*, who though accomplished in all the vertues required in a Prince, was by the general Assembly of the Estate at *Blois* declared uncapable of Succession to the Crown of *France*, for being a Protestant. And notwithstanding his Valour, Industry, Reputation and Power, increased by gaining four great Battels, yet he could never be admitted King, till he had renounced the Religion that was his obstacle. And *Sigismund*, Son of *John* of *Sweden*, King of that Country by Inheritance, and of *Poland* by Election, was deprived of his Hereditary Crown, and his Children disinherited only for being a Papist, and acting conformably to the Principles of that Religion, though in all other respects he deserved to be a King, and was most acceptable unto the Nation.

But if ever this Maxim deserved to be considered, surely it was in the case of the Duke of *York*. The violence of his natural temper is sufficiently known: His vehemency in exalting the Prerogative (in his Brothers time) beyond its due bounds, and the Principles of his Religion, which carry him to all imaginable excesses of cruelty, have convinced all mankind that he must be excluded, or the Name of King being left unto him, the power put into the hands of another. The Parliament therefore considering this, and observing the Precedents of former Ages, did wisely chuse rather to exclude him, than to leave him the Name, and place the Power in a Regent. For they
could

could not but look upon it as Folly, to expect that one of his temper, bred up in such Principles in Politicks, as made him in love with Arbitrary Power, and bigotted in that Religion, which always propagates it self by Blood, would patiently bear these shackles, which would be very disguftful unto a Prince of the most meek disposition. And would he not thereby have been provok'd to the utmost Fury and Revenge against those who laid them upon him? This would certainly have bred a Contest, and these limitations of Power proposed to keep up the Government, must unavoidably have destroyed it, or the Nation (which necessity would have forced into a War in its own natural defence) must have perished either by it, or with it. The Success of such Controversies are in the hand of God, but they are undertaken upon too unequal terms, when the People by Victory can gain no more, than what without hazard may be done by Law, and would be ruin'd if it should fall out otherwise. The Duke with Papists might then make such a Peace, as the *Romans* are said to have made once in our desolated Country, by the slaughter of all the Inhabitants able to make War, *& ubi solitudinem faciunt, pacem appellant*. This is the happy state *Tacit.* they present unto us, who condemn the Parliament for bringing in a Bill of Exclusion. This is the way to have such a Peace as the *Spaniards*, for the propagation of the Gospel, made in the *West-Indies*, at the instigation of the Jesuits, who govern'd their Councils. And seeing they have the Duke no less under their power and directions, we may easily believe they would put him upon the same Methods. But as it is not to be imagined, that any Nation that hath vertue, courage and strength equal unto the *English*, will so tamely expect their ruine; so the passing a Bill to exclude him, may avoid, but cannot (as the Declaration phraseth it) establish a War. But if there must be a War, let it be under the Authority of Law, let it be against a banished, excluded Pretender. There is no fear of the consequence of such a War : No true *Englishman* can join with him, or countenance his Usurpation after this Act; and for his Popish and foreign Adherents, they will neither be more provok'd, nor more powerful by the passing of it. Nor will his Exclusion make it at all *necessary to maintain a standing Force for preserving the Government, and the Peace of the Kingdom.* The whole People will be an Army for that purpose, and every

Heart:

Heart and Hand, will be prepared to maintain that so neceffary, so much defired Law : A Law for which three Parliaments have been so earneft with his Majefty, not only in purfuance of their own Judgments, but by the direction of thofe that fent them. It was the univerfal opinion of the Papifts, that *Mary* Queen of *Scots* was excluded only by an Act of Parliament, and yet we fee Queen *Elizabeth* reigned glorioufly and peaceably forty years without any ftanding force. But our Minifters do but diffemble with us, when they pretend to be fo much afraid of a ftanding Army. We know how eagerly they have defired, and how often they attempted to eftablifh one. We have feen two Armies raifed with no other defign, as has been fince undeniably proved ; and one of thofe they were fo loth to part with, that more than one Act of Parliament was neceffary to get it disbanded. And fince that, they have increafed the Guards to fuch a degree, that they are become a formidable ftanding Force. A thing fo odious to a free People, that the raifing of one fingle Regiment in *Spain*, within thefe fix years, under colour of being a Guard for the King's Perfon, fo inflam'd the Nation, that a Rebellion had enfued, if they had not been disbanded fpeedily. The Nobility and Gentry of that Kingdom looking upon themfelves as their Kings natural Guard, fcorned that fo honourable a Name fhould be given to Mercenaries.

But as His Majefty was perfwaded to refolve againft the expedient propofed, to fecure our Peace by excluding the Duke, fo it is evident, that nothing was intended by thofe other ways which were darkly and dubioufly intimated in His Majefties Speech unto the Parliament at *Oxford*, and repeated in the Declaration ; and His Majefty in his Wifdom could not but know that they fignified nothing. And thofe who fpake more plainly, in propofing a Regency as an Expedient, did in publick and private declare, they believed the Duke would not confent unto it, nor unto any unufual reftriction of the Royal Power. So that they could have no other defign therein, than a plaufible pretence to delude the Parliament and People. Some fuch confideration induced them to revive the diftinction between the King's perfonal and politick capacity, by feparating the power from the perfon, which we have reafon to believe they efteemed unfeafable. However, it is more than probable that the *Je-*
fuites

fuites, *Cafuifts*, and Popifh Lawyers would reject it, as well as any thing elfe that might preferve us from falling under his power. And the *Pope*, who could abfolve King *John*, *Henry* the third and others, from the Oaths they had taken, to preferve the Rights and Liberties of their Subjects, might with the fame facility diffolve any that the Duke would take. And as our Hiftories teftifie what bloody Wars were thereby brought upon the Nation, we have reafon to believe, that if the like fhould again happen, it would be more fatal unto us, when Religion is concerned, which was not then in queftion. Would not his *Confeffor* foon convince him, that all Laws made in favour of Herefie are void? And would he not be liable to the heavieft Curfes, if he fuffered his Power to be ufed againft his Religion? The little regard he hath to Laws whilft a Subject, is enough to inftruct us what refpect he would bear to them if he fhould be King. Shall we therefore fuffer the Royal Dignity to defcend on him, who hath made ufe of all the Power he has been entrufted with hitherto, for our deftruction? And who fhall execute this great Truft? The next Heir may be an Infant, or one willing to furrender it into his hands. But fhould it be otherwife, yet ftill there is no hope of having any fruit of this Expedient without a War, and to be obliged to fwear Allegiance to a Popifh Prince, to own his Title, to acknowledge him Supreme Head of the Church, and Defender of the Faith, feems a very ftrange way of entitling our felves to fight againft him.

The two Reafons which the Declaration pretends to give againft the Exclufion, are certainly of more force againft the Expedient. *A ftanding Force* would have been abfolutely *neceffary*, to have plac'd and kept the *Adminiftration in Proteftant hands*; *and the Monarchy it felf had been deftroy'd by a Law*, which was to have taken all forts of Power from the King, and made him not fo much as a Duke of *Venice*. How abfurdly and incoherently do thefe men difcourfe! Sometimes the Government is fo Divine a thing, that no human Law can leffen or take away his Right, who only pretends in Succeffion, and is at prefent but a Subject: But at other times they tell us of Acts of Parliament to banifh him out of his own Dominions, to deprive him of all Power, of his whole Kingfhip after he fhall be in poffeffion of the Throne. The cheat of this Expedient appear'd fo grofs in the Houfe of Commons, that one of the Dukes pro-

E   feffed

feſſed Vaſſals, who had a little more Honour than the reſt, was aſham'd of it, and openly renounced the Project which they had been forming ſo long, and thought they had ſo artificially diſguiſed. But though it was ſo well expoſed in the Houſe, yet the Miniſters thought the men without doors might be ſtill deceived, and therefore they do not bluſh to value themſelves again upon it in their Declaration.

As for the Inſinuation which follows, That there was reaſon to believe that *the Parliament would have paſſed further to attempt other great and important Changes at preſent:* If it be meant any Change of the Conſtitution of the Government, 'tis a malicious ſuggeſtion of thoſe men, who are ever inſtilling into His Majeſty's mind ill thoughts of his Parliament, ſince no Vote nor Propoſition in either Houſe could give any ground for ſuch ſuſpicion, and therefore in this matter the people may juſtly accuſe the Court, (who ſo often cry out againſt them for it) of being moved by cauſeleſs Fears and Jealouſies. And for His Majeſty to be perſwaded to arraign the whole Body of his People, upon the ill-grounded ſurmiſes, or malicious and falſe ſuggeſtions of evil and corrupt men about him, doth neither well become the Juſtice of a Prince, nor is agreeable to the meaſures of Wiſdom, which he ſhould Govern Himſelf, as well as Rule his People by. And if an attendance to the ſlandrous Accuſations of perſons, who hate Parliaments, becauſe their Crimes are ſuch that they have reaſon to fear them, govern and ſway his Royal Mind, there can never want grounds for the Diſſolution of any Parliaments. But if they mean *by attempting great and important Changes,* that they would have beſought his Majeſty that the Duke might no longer have the Government in his hands, that his Dependents ſhould no longer preſide in his Councils, no longer poſſeſs all the great Truſts and Offices in the Kingdom; that our Ports, our Garriſons, and our Fleets, ſhould be no longer governed by ſuch as are at his Devotion, that Characters of Honour and Favour ſhould be no longer plac'd on men that the Wiſdom of the Nation hath judged to be Favourers of Popery, or Penſioners of *France.* Theſe were indeed *great and important Changes,* but ſuch as it becomes *Engliſh* men to believe were deſigned by that Parliament; ſuch as will be deſigned and preſt for by every Parliament, and ſuch as the people will ever pray may at laſt find ſucceſs with the King. Without theſe thefe *Charges*, the Bill of Exclufion would only provoke, not difa'm our Enemies', nay the very Money which we muft have paid for it, would have been made ufe of to fecure and haften the Dukes return upon us.

We are now come to the Confideration of that only fault which was peculiar to the Parliament at *Oxford*, and that was their behaviour in Relation to the bufinefs of *Fitz-Harris*. The Declaration fays, *he was impeached of High-Treafon by the Commons*, and they had caufe to think his Treafons to be of fuch an extraordinary Nature, that they well deferved an Examination in Parliament. For *Fitz-Harris*, a known *Irifh* Papift, appear'd by the Informations given in the Houfe, to be made ufe of by fome very great Perfons to fet up a counterfeit Proteftant Confpiracy, and thereby not only to drown the noife of the Popifh Plot, but to take off the Heads of the moft eminent of thofe, who ftill refufed to bow their Knees to *Baal*. There had been divers fuch honeft Contrivances before, which had unluckily fail'd, but the principal Contrivers avoided the Difcovery, as the others did the Punifhment; in what manner, and by what helps, the whole Nation is now pretty fenfible. Being warned by this experience, they grew more Cautious than ever, and therefore that the Treafon which they were to fet on Foot, might look as unlike a Popifh defign as was poffible, they fram'd a Libel full of the moft bitter Invictives againft Popery and the Duke of *York*. It carried as much feeming zeal for the Proteftant Religion, as *Coleman*'s *Declaration*, and as much care and concern for our Laws, as the *Penners* of this *Declaration* would feem to have. But it was alfo filled with the moft fubtil Infinuations, and the fharpeft Expreffions againft His Majefty that could be invented, and with direct and paffionate Incitements to Rebellion. This Paper was to be conveyed by unknown Meffengers, to their hands who were to be betray'd, and then they were to be feized upon, and thofe Libels found about tham, were to be a Confirmation of the Truth of a Rebellion, which they had provided Witneffes to Swear was defigned by the Proteftants, and had before prepared Men to believe by private Whifpers. And the credit of this Plot fhould no doubt have been foon confirmed, by fpeedy Juftice done upon the pretended Criminals. But as well laid as this Contrivance feem to be, yet it fpoke it felf to be of a Popifh Extraction. 'Tis a policy the Jefuits have often ufed,

to

to divert a ftorm which was falling upon themfelves. Accordingly heretofore they had prepared both Papers and Witneffes, to have made the *Puritans* guilty of the Gunpowder Treafon, had it fucceeded as they hoped for.

The hainous Nature of the Crime, and the greatnefs of the Perfons fuppofed to be concern'd, deferved an extraordinary Examination, with a Jury, who were only to enquire whether *Fitz-Harris* was guilty of framing that Libel, he could never make; and the Commons believed none but the Parliament was big enough to go through with. They took notice that the Zeal and Courage of inferior Courts was abated, and that the Judges at the Tryal of *Wakeman* and *Gafcoign* (however it came to pafs) behaved themfelves very unlike the fame Men they were, when others of the Plotters had been Tryed. They had not forgot another Plot of this Nature difcovered by *Dangerfield*, which tho plainly proved to the Council, yet was quite ftifled by the great Diligence of the *Kings Bench*, which rendred him as an incompetent Witnefs. Nor did they only fear the perverfion of Juftice, but the Mifapplication of Mercy too. For they had feen that the Mouths of *Gadbury* and others, as foon as they began to confefs, were fuddenly ftopt by a gracious Pardon. And they were more Jealous than ordinary in this cafe, becaufe when *Fitz-Harris* was inclined to Repentance, and had begun a Confeffion, to the furprize of the whole Kingdom, without any vifible caufe, he was taken out of the lawful Cuftody of the Sheriffs, and fhut up a clofe Prifoner in the *Tower*. The Commons therefore had no other way to be fecure that the Profecution fhould be effectual, the Judgment indifferent, and the Criminal out of all hopes of a Pardon (unlefs by an ingenuous Confeffion he could engage both Houfes in a powerful Mediation to His Majefty in his behalf) but by impeaching of him. They were fure no Pardon could ftop their Suit, tho the King might releafe his own Profecution by his Pardon.

Hitherto the Proceedings of the Commons in this Bufinefs could not be liable to Exception, for that they might lawfully Impeach any Commoner before the Lords, was yet never doubted. The Lords themfelves had agreed that point, when the day before they had fent down the Plea of Sir *William Scroggs* to an Impeachment of Treafon, then depending before them.

And

And they are men of ftrange confidence, who at this time of day take upon them to deny a Jurifdiction of the Lords, which hath been practifed in all times without controul, and fuch a fundamental of the Government, that there could be no fecurity without it. Were it otherwife, it would be in the power of the King, by making Commoners Minifters of State, to fubvert the Government by their Contrivances when he pleafed : Their Greatnefs would keep them out of the reach of ordinary Courts of Juftice, and their Treafons might not perhaps be within the Statutes, but fuch as fall under the cognizance of no other Court than the Parliament ; and if the People might not of Right demand Juftice there, they might without fear of punifhment, act the moft deftructive Villanies againft the Kingdom.

As a Remedy againft this Evil, the *Mirrour of Juftice* tells us, *that Parliaments were ordained to hear and determine all Complaints of wrongful Acts, done by the King, Queen, or their Children, and fuch others againft whom common Right cannot be had elfewhere.* Which as to the King, is no otherwife to be underftood, than that if he err by Illegal Perfonal Commands or Orders, he is to be admonifhed by Parliament, and addreffed unto for Remedy ; but all others being but Subjects, are to be punifhed by Parliaments, according to the Laws of Parliaments. Cap. 1. Sect. 2. pag. 9.

If the ends were well confidered for which Parliaments were ordained, as they are declared in the Statute ; *Item for maintenance of the faid Articles and Statutes,* (*viz.* Magna Charta, &c.) a Parliament fhall be holden every year, by them as well as by the foregoing ancient Authority, none could be deceived by the Parliament *Rol.* of 4 *Ed.* 3. where it is mentioned as accorded between the King and his Grands , (that is, his Lords) that Judgment of Death, given by the Peers againft Sir *Simon de Beresford, Matrever,* and others, upon the Murther of King *Ed.* 2. and his Uncle, fhould not be drawn into Example, whereby the Peers might be charged to judge others than their Peers, *contrary to the Law of the Land, if fuch a Cafe fhould happen.* For whereas from this Record fome would perfwade us that the Lords are difcharged from judging Commoners, and that our ancient Government is alter'd in this Cafe by that Record, which they fay is an Act of Parliament. 36 Ed. 3. 10. Rot. Parl. 4 Ed. 3. Nu 6.

The

The ftile and form of it is fo different from that which is ufed in
Acts of Parliament, that many are inclined t● believe it to be no
other thing, than an agreement between the King and the Lords.
But to remove all future fcruples in the Cafe, let it be admitted to
be an Act of Parliament, and if there be nothing accorded in it,
to acquit the Lords from trying Commoners Impeached before
them by the Commons in Parliament, then we hope that fhame
will ftop their mouths, who have made fuch a noife againft the
Commons with this Record. *Firft*, It is evident from the Roll
it felf, with other Records, that the Lords did judg thofe Commoners contrary to the Law of the Land, that is, at the inftance of the King, and the Profecution of their Enemies, without the due courfe of the Law; or calling them to make their
Defence, and (for ought appears) without legal Teftimony.
Secondly, It is evident, that they were driven upon this illegal
Proceeding, by the Power and Authority of the King, and fome
Profecutors, who earneftly preffed the Lords thereunto, upon
pretence of fpeedily avenging the Blood of the former King
and his Uncle. So that the Judgment was given at the Kings
Suit, in a way not warranted by the Law and Cuftom of Parliament, or any other Law of the Kingdom. Surely when the
Lords blood was fuffered to cool, they had reafon to defire
fomething might be left upon Record, to preferve them for the
future from being put upon fuch fhameful Work, tho fuch a
cafe as the Murder of a King fhould again happen, as it feems
they did not fear to be preffed in any other, fo to violate the
Laws. But *Thirdly*, There is not a word in the Record, that
imports a reftriction of that lawful Jurifdiction, which our Conftitution placeth in the Lords to try Commoners, when their
Cafes fhould come before them lawfully, at the Suit of the Commons by Impeachment. There is no mark of an Intention to
change any part of the Ancient Government, but to provide
againft the Violation of it, and that the Law might ftand as before notwithftanding the unlawful Judgment they had lately
given. So that the queftion is ftill the fame, Whether by the
Law of the Land, that is the Law and Cuftom of Parliament, or
any other Law, the Lords ought to try Commoners Impeached
by the Commons in Parliament, as if that Record had never
been. And we cannot think that any man of Sence, will from
that Record make an argument in this point, fince it could be no

better than to infer, that becaufe the Lords are no more to be
preffed by the King, or at his Suit, to give Judgment againft
Commoners contrary to the Law of the Land, when they are not
Impeached in Parliament, therefore they muft give no Judgment againft them at the Suit of the Commons in Parliament,
when they are by them Impeached, according to the Laws and
Cuftoms of Parliament. But if fuch as delight in thefe Cavils had
fearched into all the Records relating unto that of the 4 *Ed.* 3.
they might have found in the 19th of the fame King a Writ
iffued out to fufpend the Execution of the Judgment againft *Ma-*
trevers, becaufe it had been illegally paffed. And the chief
reafon therein given is, that he had not been Impeached, and fuffered to make his Defence. But it was never fuggefted nor imagined that the Lords that judged him, had no Jurifdiction over
him becaufe he was a Commoner, or ought not to have exer-
cifed it, if he had been Impeached ; nor was it pretended that
by *Magna Charta* he ought to have been tried only by his Peers ;
the Laws of the Land therein mentioned, and the Laws and
Cuftoms of Parliaments, being better known and more reve-
renced in thofe days, than to give way to fuch a miftake. They
might alfo have found by another Record of the 26th of the
fame King, that by undoubted Act of Parliament, *Matrevers*
was pardon'd, and the Judgment is therein agreed by the Lords
and Commons to have been illegal, and unjuftly paffed, by
the violent Profecution of his Enemies; but it is not alledged
that it was *coram non judice*, as if the Lords might not have judged him, if the proceedings before them had been legal. But as
the fenfe and proceedings of all Parliaments have ever been beft
known by their practice, the Objectors might have found by
all the Records fince the 4 *Ed.* 3. that Commoners as well as
Lords might be, and have been, Impeached before Lords, and
judged by them to Capital or other Punifhments, as appears
undeniably to every man that hath read our Hiftories or Records. And verily the concurrent fenfe and practice of Parliaments for fo many Ages, will be admitted to be a better in-
terpretation of their own Acts, than the fenfe that thefe men
have lately put upon them to increafe our Diforders. But to
filence the moft malicious in this point, let the famous Act of
the 25 of *Ed.* 3. be confidered, which hath ever fince limi-
ted all inferior Courts in their Jurifdiction, unto the Trial of

Rot. Parl.
19 *Ed.* 3.
M. 18.

Rot. Parl.
26 *Ed.* 3.
M. 25.

fuch

such Treasons only as are therein particularly specified, and reserved all other Treasons to the Trial and Judgment of Parliament. So that if any such be committed by Commoners, they must be so Tried, or not at all. And if the last should be allowed, it will follow, that the same fact which in a Peer is Treason, and punishable with Death, in a Commoner is no Crime, and subject to no punishment.

Nor doth *Magna Charta* confine all Trials to common Juries, for it ordains that they should be tried by *the Judgment of Peers*, *or by the Law of the Land*. And will any man say the Law of Parliament is not the Law of the Land ? Nor are these words in *Magna Charta* superfluous or insignificant, for then there would be no Trial before the *Constable* or *Marshal*, where there is no Jury at all ; there could be no Trial of a Peer of the Realm upon an Appeal of Murther, who according to the Law ought in such cases to be try'd by a common Jury, and not by his Peers. And since the Records of Parliaments are full of Impeachment of Commons, and no instance can be given of the rejection of any such Impeachment, it is the Commons who have reason to cite *Magna Charta* upon this occasion, which provides expresly against the denial of Justice. And indeed it looks like a denial of Justice, when a Court that hath undoubted cognizance of a Cause regularly brought before them, shall refuse to hear it : but most especially when (as in this case) the Prosecutors could not be so in any other Court, so as a final stop was put to their Suit, though the Lords could not judicially know whether any body else would prosecute elsewhere.

o. 2. Inst. 9.

This Proceeding of the Lords looks the more odly, because they rejected the Cause, before they knew as Judges what it was, and *referred it to the ordinary course of Law*, without staying to hear whether it were a matter whereof an inferior Court could take cognizance. There are Treasons which can only be adjudged in Parliament, and if we may collect the sense of the House of Commons from their Debates, they thought there was a mixture of those kind of Treasons in *Fitz-Harris*'s Case. And therefore there was little reason for that severe suggestion, *that the Impeachment was only designed to delay a Trial*, since a compleat Examination of his Crime could be had no where but in Parliament. But it seems somewhat strange, *that the delaying of a Trial, and that against a professed Papist charged with Trea-*

son,

son, should be a matter so extremely sensible: For might it not be well retorted by the people, That it had been long *a matter extremely sensible to them*, that so many Prorogations, so many Dissolutions, so many other Arts had been used to delay the Trials, which his Majesty had often desired, and the Parliament prepared for, against *Five professed Popish Lords charged with Treasons of an extraordinary nature.* But above all, that it was a matter *extremely sensible* to the whole Kingdom, to see such Unparliamentary and mean sollicitations, used to promote this pretended Rejection of the Commons Accusation, as are not fit to be remembred. 'Tis there that the *delay of the Trials is to be laid*; for had the Impeachment been proceeded upon, and the Parliament suffered to sit, *Fitz-Harris* had been long since Executed, or deserved Mercy by a full Discovery of the secret Authors of these malicious Designs against the King and People. For though the Declaration says a *Trial was directed*, yet we are sure nothing was done in order to it, till above a month after the Dissolution. And it hath since raised such Questions, as we may venture to say were never talk'd of before in *Westminster-Hall*; Questions which touch the Judicature of the Lords, and the Privileges of the Commons in such a degree, that they will never be determined by the decision of any inferior Court, but will assuredly at one time or other have a farther Examination.

We have seen now that the Commons did it not without some ground, when they Voted *the refusal of the Lords to proceed upon an Impeachment, to be a denial of Justice, and a violation of the Constitution of Parliaments* ; and the second Vote was but an application of this Opinion to the present Case. The third Vote made upon that occcasion was no more than what the King himself had allowed, and all the Judges of *England* had agreed to be Law, in the Case of the Five Impeached Lords, who were only generally impeached, and the Parliament dissolved, before any Articles were sent up against them. Yet they had been first indicted in an inferior Court, and preparations made for their Trial ; but the Judges thought at that time, that a Prosecution of all the Commons was enough to stop all Prosecutions of an inferior nature. The Commons had not impeached *Fitz-Harris*, but that they judged his Case required so publick an Examination; and for any other Court to go about to Try and Condemn him, tho' it should be granted to be for another Crime, is as far as in them lies to stifle that Examination.

F   By

By this time every man will begin to queftion, whether *the Lords did Themfelves or the Commons Right, in the refufing to countenance fuch a Proceeding?* But one of the Penmen of this Declaration has done Himfelf and the Nation Right, and has difcovered himfelf by ufing his ordinary phrafe upon this occafion. The Perfon is well known without naming him, who always tells men they have done themfelves no Right, when he is refolved to do them none. As for the Commons, nothing was *carried on to extremity by them*, nothing done but what was Parliamentary: They could not defire a Conference, till they had firft ftated their own Cafe, and afferted by Votes the matter which they were to maintain at a Conference. And fo far were thofe Votes from putting the Two Houfes *beyond a poffibility of Reconciliation*, that they were made in order to it, and there was no other way to attain it. And fo far was the Houfe of Commons from thinking themfelves to be out of a capacity of tranfacting with the Lords any farther, that they were preparing to fend a Meffage for a Conference to accomodate this Difference, at the very inftant that the Black Rod called them to their Diffolution. If every difference in Opinion or Vote fhould be faid to put the Two Houfes *out of capacity of tranfacting bufinefs together*, every Parliament almoft muft be diffolved as foon as called. However our Minifters might know well enough, that *there was no poffibility of reconciling the Two Houfes*, becaufe they had before refolved *to put them out of a capacity of tranfacting together, by a fudden Diffolution*. But that very thing juftifies the Commons to the World, who cannot but perceive that there was folemn and good ground for them to defire an enquiry into *Fitz-Harris's* Treafon, fince they who influence our Affairs were fo ftartl'd at it, that, in order to prevent it, they firft promoted this Difference between the Two Houfes, and then broke the Parliament left it fhould be compofed.

There is another thing which muft not be paft over without Obfervation, That the Minifters in this Paper take upon them to decide this great Difpute between the Two Houfes, and to give judgment on the fide of the Lords. We may well demand what perfon is by our Law conftituted a Judge of their Privileges, or hath Authority to cenfure the Votes of one Houfe, made with reference to matters wherein they were contefting with the other Houfe, *as the greateft violation of the Conftitution of Parliaments?*

liaments ? They ought certainly to have excepted the power which is here aſſumed of giving ſuch a Judgment, and publiſhing ſuch a Charge, as being not only the higheſt Violation of the Conſtitution, but directly tending to the deſtruction of it.

This was the Caſe, *and a few days continuance being like to pro-duce a good underſtanding between the Two Houſes*, to the advancing *all thoſe* great and *publick ends*, for which the Nation hop'd they were called, the Miniſters *found it* neceſſary to put an end to that Parliament likewiſe.

We have followed the Writers of the Declaration through the ſeveral parts of it, wherein the Houſe of Commons are Reproached with any particular Miſcarriages, and now they come to ſpeak more at large, and to give Caution againſt two ſorts of ill Men. One ſort they ſay, *Are men fond of their old beloved Commonwealth Principles* ; *and others are angry at being diſappoint-ed in deſigns they had for accompliſhing their own Ambition and Greatneſs*. Surely, if they know any ſuch Perſons, the only way to have prevented the miſchiefs which they pretend to fear from them, had been to have diſcovered them, and ſuffered the Parliament to Sit to provide againſt the Evils they would bring upon the Nation, by proſecuting of them. But if they mean by theſe lovers of *Commonwealth Principles* , men paſſio-nately devoted to the Publick good, and to the common Service of their Country, who believe that Kings were inſtituted for the good of the People, and Government ordained for the ſake of thoſe that are to be governed , and therefore complain or grieve when it is uſed to contrary ends, every Wiſe and Honeſt man will be proud to be ranked in that number. And if *Com-monwealth* ſignifies the common Good, in which ſence it hath in all Ages been uſed by all good Authors, and which *Bodin* puts upon it, when he ſpeaks of the Government of *France*, which he calls a *Republick*, no good man will be aſham'd of it. Our own Authors, *The Mirror of Juſtice*, *Bracton*, *Fleta*, *Forteſcue*, and others in former times. And of latter years, Sir *Thomas Smith*, Secretary of State in the Reign of Queen *Elizabeth*, in his Diſcourſes of the Commonwealth of *England*, Sir *Francis Bacon*, *Cook*, and others, take it in the ſame Senſe. And not only divers of our Statutes uſe the Word, but even King *James* in his firſt Speech unto the Parliament, acknowledgeth himſelf to be the *Servant* of the *Commonwealth*; and King *Charles* the I.

both

both before and in the time of the War, never expreſſeth himſelf otherwiſe. To be *fond* therefore of ſuch *Commonwealth
Principles*, becomes every *Engliſhman*; and the whole Kingdom
did hope, and were afterwards glad to find, they had ſent ſuch
Men to Parliament. But if the Declaration would intimate,
that there had been any deſign of ſetting up a *Demccratial* Government, in Oppoſition to our legal *Monarchy*, it is a Calumny
juſt of a piece with the other things which the penners of this
Declaration have vented, in order to the laying upon others the
blame of a deſign to overthrow the Government, which only
belongs unto themſelves.

It is ſtrange how this *Wcrd*, ſhould ſo change its ſignification,
with us in the ſpace of twenty years. All *Monarchies* in the
World, that are not purely Barbarous and Tyrannical, have
ever been called *Commonwealths*. *Rome* it ſelf altered not that
Name, when it fell under the Sword of the *Cæfars*. The proudeſt
and cruelleſt of Emperors diſdained it not. And in our days, it
doth not only belong to *Venice*, *Genoua*, *Switzerland*, and the
United Provinces of the *Netherlands*, but to *Germany,Spain,France,
Sweden, Poland*, and all the Kingdoms of *Europe*. May it not
therefore be apprehended that our preſent Miniſters, who have
ſo much decried this *Wurd* ſo well known to our Laws, ſo often
uſed by our beſt Writers, and by all our Kings until this day, are
Enemies to the thing? And that they who make it a brand of
Infamy to be of *Commonwealth Principles*, that is, devoted to the
good of the People, do intend no other than the hurt and miſ-
chief of that People? Can they in plainer terms declare their
fondneſs of their *beloved* Arbitrary Power, and their deſign to ſet
it up, by ſubverting our Ancient Legal Monarchy, inſtituted for
the benefit of the Commonwealth, than by thus caſting reproach
upon thoſe who endeavour to uphold it ?

Let the Nation then to whom the Appeal is made, judg
who are the men that endeavour to *Poiſon* the People, and who
they are who are guilty of deſigning Innovations. *Bracton*
tells us, that *poteſtas Regis*, is *poteſtas Legis*: It is from the
Law that he hath his Power; it is by the Law that he is King,
and for the good of the People by whoſe conſent it is made.
The Liberty and welfare of a great Nation, was of too much
importance to be ſuffered to depend upon the will of one Man.
The beſt and wiſeſt might be tranſported by an exceſs of Power truſted with them; and the experience of all times ſhoweth,
that

that Princes,as men,are fubject to Errors, and might be mifled. Therefore (as far as mansWit could forefee) our Conftitution hath provided
by annual Parliaments, 36 *Edw.* 3. cap. 10. that the Commonwealth
might receive no hurt ; and it is the Parliament, that muft from time
to time correct the mifchiefs which daily creep in upon us. Let us then
no longer wonder, when we fee fuch frequent Prorogations and Diffo-
lutions of Parliaments ; nor ftand amazed at this laft unparallell'd ef-
fort of the Minifters, by this Declaration to render two Parliaments odious unto the people. They well know that Parliaments were ordain'd
to prevent fuch mifchiefs as they defign'd, and if they were fuffered
to purfue the ends of their Inftitution, would endeavour to preferve all
things in their due order. To unite the King unto his People, and the
hearts of the People unto the King ; to keep the Regal Authority within the bounds of Law, and perfwade his Majefty to direct it to the publick Good, which the Law intends. But as this is repugnant to the in-
troduction of Arbitrary Power and Popery, they who delight in both
cannot but hate it, and choofe rather to bring matters into fuch a ftate
as may fuit with their private Interefts, than fuffer it to continue in its
right Channel. They love to fifh in troubl'd Waters, and they find all
Diforders profitable unto themfelves. They can flatter the humor of a
mifguided Prince, and increafe their Fortunes by the exceffes of a waft-
ful Prodigal ; the frenzy of an imperious Woman is eafily rendred pro-
pitious unto them, and they can turn the Zeal of a violent Bigot to their
advantage ; the Treacheries of falfe Allies agree with their own cor-
ruptions; and as they fear nothing fo much as that the King fhould return unto his People, and keep all things quiet, they almoft ever render themfelves fubfervient to fuch as would difturb them. And if thefe
two laft Parliaments, according to their Duty, and the Truft repofed
in them, have more fteddily than any other before them perfifted in the
pious and juft endeavours of eafing the Nation of any of its Grievances,
the Authors of the Declaration found it was their beft courfe, by falfe
colours put upon things, and fubtil mifreprefentations of their actings,
to delude the People into an abhorrence of their own Reprefentatives ;
but with what candor and ingenuity they have attempted it, is already
fufficiently made known. And if we look about us, we fhall find thofe
who defign a Change on either hand fomenting a mifunderftanding between the King, his Parliament and People, whilft perfons who love the
legal Monarchy both out of choice and confcience, are they who defire
the frequent and fuccefsful meetings of the Great Council of the Nation.

As for the other fort of peevifh men, of whom the Declaration gives
us warning, *who are angry at the difappointment of their ambitious De-*
figns,

signs; if thefe words are intended to reflect on thofe men of Honour and Confcience, who being qualified for the higheft employments of State, have either left, or refufed, or been removed from them, becaufe they would not accept or retain them at the price of felling their Country, and Enflaving pofterity: And who are content to Sacrifice their fafety as well as their intereft for the publick, and expofe themfelves to the malice of the men in power, and to the daily Plots, Perjuries, and Subornations of the Papifts. I fay, if thefe be the *ambitious men* fpoken of, the people will have confideration for what they fay, and therefore it will be wifdom, to give fuch men as thefe no occafion to fay, that they intend to *lay afide the ufe of Parliaments.*

In good earneft, the behaviour of the Minifters of late, gives but too juft occafion to fay, that the *ufe of Parliaments is already laid afide.* For tho His Majefty has owned in fo many of His Speeches and Declarations, the great danger of the Kingdom, and the neceffity of the Aid and Counfel of Parliaments, he hath neverthelefs been prevailed upon to Diffolve four in the fpace of 26 Months, without making provifion by their advice fuitable to our dangers or wants. Nor can we hope the Court will ever love any Parliament better, than the firft of thofe four, wherein they had fo dearly purchafed fuch a number of faft Friends ; Men who having firft fold themfelves, would not ftick to fell any thing after. And we may well fufpect they mean very ill at Court, when their defigns fhock't fuch a Parliament. For that very *Favourite* Parliament no fooner began in good earneft to examine what had been done, and what was doing, but they were fent away in hafte, and in a fright, though the Minifters know they loft thereby a conftant Revenue of extraordinary Supplies. And are the Minifters at prefent more innocent, than at that time? The fame intereft hath the afcendant at Court ftill, and they have heightned the Refentments of the Nation, by repeated affronts ; and can we believe them that they dare fuffer a Parliament now to Sit?

But we have gain'd at leaft this one Point by the Declaration, that it is own'd to us, *that Parliaments are the beft Method, for healing the diftempers of the Kingdom, and the only means to preferve the Monarchy in credit both at home and abroad.* Own'd by thefe very men who have fo malicioufly rendred many former Parliaments ineffectual, and by this Declaration have done their utmoft to make thofe which are to come as fruitlefs, and thereby have confeffed that they have no concern for *healing the diftempers of the Kingdom, and preferving the credit of the Monarchy* ; which is in effect to acknowledge themfelves, to be what the

Com-

Commons called them, *Enemies to the King and Kingdom.* Nothing can be more true, than that the Kingdom can never recover its *strength and reputation abroad,* or its ancient Peace and Settlement at home, His Majesty can never be relieved from his fears and his domestick wants, nor secure from the Affronts which he daily suffers from abroad, till he resolves not only to *call Parliaments,* but to Hearken to them when they are called. For without that, it is not a Declaration, it is not repeated promises, nay it is not the frequent calling of Parliaments which will convince the world, that the *use of them is not intended to be laid aside.*

However we rejoyce, that his Majesty seems *resolved to have frequent Parliaments,* and hope he will be just to Himself, and us, by continuing constant to this Resolution. Yet we cannot but doubt in some degree, when we remember the Speech made 26 *Jan.* 1679 to both Houses, wherein he told them, that he was *Unalterably of an Opinion, that long intervals of Parliaments were absolutely necessary, for composing and quieting the minds of the People.* Therefore which ought we rather to believe, the *Speech* or the *Declaration?* or which is likely to last longest, a *Resolution* or *an unalterable opinion,* is a matter too Nice for any but Court-Criticks to Decide. The effectual performance of the last part of the promise, will give us assurance of the first. When we see the real fruits of these *utmost endeavours to extirpate Popery out of Parliament ;* when we see the D. of *York* no longer first Minister, or rather protector of these Kingdoms, and his Creatures no longer to have the whole direction of Affairs; when we see that Love to our Religion and Laws is no longer a crime at Court ; no longer a certain forerunner of being Disgrac'd and Remov'd from all Offices and Employments in their Power ; when the word Loyal (which is faithful to the Law, shall be restored to its old meaning, and no longer signifie one who is for subverting the Laws; When we see the Commissions fill'd with hearty Protestants, and the Laws executed in good earnest against the Papists; the Discoverers of the Plot countenanc'd, or at least heard, and suffered to give their Evidence; the Courts of Justice steady, and not Avowing a Jurisdiction one day, which they disown the next ; no more Grand Juries discharg'd, left they should hear Witnesses ; nor Witnesses hurried away, left they should inform Grand Juries ; when we see no more Instruments from Court labouring to raise Jealousies of Protestants at home, and some regard had to Protestants abroad ; when we observe somewhat else to be meant by *Governing according to Law,* than barely to put in Execution against Dissenters, the Laws made against Papists; then we shall promise our selves not only *frequent Parliaments,* but all the blessed effects of pursuing Parliamentary Councels, the

Extir-

(48)

Extirpation of Popery, the Redrefs of Grievances , the flourifhing of Laws, and the perfeƈt Reftoring the Monarchy to the Credit, which it ought to have (but which the Authors of the Declaration confefs it wants) *both at Home and Abroad.* There needs no time *to open the Eyes of His Majefties good Subjeƈts, and their Hearts are ready prepared to meet him in Parliament, in order to perfeƈt all the good Settlement and Peace, wanting in Church and State.*

But whilft there are fo many little Emiffaries imployed to fow and encreafe Divifions in the Nation, as if the Minifters had a mind to make His Majefty the Head of a Faƈtion, and joyn himfelf to one Party in the Kingdom, who has a juft right of Governing all (which *Thuanus lib. 28.* fays, was the notorious folly, and occafioned the Deftruƈtion of his great Grand Mother *Mary* Queen of *Scots*) whilft we fee the fame Differences promoted induftrioufly by the Court, which *gave the rife and progrefs to the late troubles,* and which were once thought fit to be buried in an Aƈt of Oblivion. Whilft we fee the Popifh Intereft fo plainly Countenanced, which was then done with Caution; when every pretence of Prerogative is ftrained to the utmoft Height; when Parliaments are ufed with contempt and indignity, and their judicature, and all their higheft Priviledges brought in queftion in Inferior Courts, we have but too good caufe to believe, that tho every Loyal and Good Man does, yet the Minifters and Favourites, do but little *confider the Rife and Progrefs of the late Troubles,* and have little *defire or care to preferve their Country from a Relapfe.* And who as they never yet fhewed *regard to Religion, Liberty or Property,* fo they would be little concern'd to fee the *Monarchy fhaken off,* if they might efcape the Vengeance of publick Juftice, due to them for fo long a Courfe of pernicious Counfels, and for Crowning all the reft of their faults by thus Refleƈting upon that High Court, before which we do not doubt but we fhall fee them one day brought to Judgment.

Thus have we with an *Englifh* plainnefs, expreffed our thoughts of the late Parliaments and their Proceedings, as well as of the Court in Relation to them, and hope this Freedom will offend no man. The Minifters, who may be concern'd through their appealing unto the People, cannot in Juftice deny unto any one of them the Liberty of weighing the Reafons which they thought fit to publifh in Vindication of their Aƈtions. But if it fhould prove otherwife, and thefe few Sheets be thought as weak and full of Errors, as thofe we endeavour to confute, or be held injurious unto them, we defire only to know in what we tranfgrefs, and that the Prefs may be open for our Juftification : Let the People to whom the Appeal is made, judg then between them and us; and let Reafon and the Law be the Rules, according unto which the Controverfy may be decided. But if by denying this, they fhall like Beafts recur to force; they will thereby acknowledg that they want the Arms which belong to rational Creatures. Whereas if the Liberty of Anfwering be left us, we will give up the Caufe, and confefs, that both Reafon and Law are wanting unto us, if we do not in our Reply fatisfy all reafonable and impartial men, that nothing is faid by us, but what is juft and neceffary, to preferve the Interefts of the King and his People. Nor can there be any thing more to the Honour of His Majefty; than to give the Nations round about us to underftand, that the King of *England*, doth neither Reign over a Bafe, Servile People, who hearing themfelves Arraign'd and Condemned, dare not fpeak in their own Defence and Vindication; nor over fo filly, foolifh and weak a People, as that ill defigned, and worfe fupported Paper might occafion the World to think, but that there are fome Perfons in his Dominions, not only of true *Englifh* Courage, but of greater intelleƈtuals as well as better Morals, than the Advifers unto, and Penners of the Declaration have manifefted themfelves to be.

F I N I S.